Conker Editions Ltd
22 Cosby Road
Littlethorpe
Leicester
LE19 2HF
Email: books@conkereditions.co.uk
Website: www.conkereditions.co.uk
First published by Conker Editions Ltd 2022
Text © 2022 Gary Silke.
Gary Silke has asserted his rights in accordance with the Copyright, Designs and Patents Act 1988 to be identified as the author of this work. All rights reserved. No part of this publication may be reproduced, stored in a retrieval system, or transmitted in any form or by any means, electronic, mechanical, photocopying, recording or otherwise, without the prior permission in writing of the publisher and the copyright owners, or as expressly permitted by law, or under terms agreed with the appropriate reprographics rights organisation. Enquiries concerning reproduction outside the terms stated here should be sent to the publishers at the UK address printed on this page.

The publisher makes no representation, express or implied, with regard to the accuracy of the information contained in this book and cannot accept any legal responsibility for any errors or omissions that may be made.

A CIP catalogue record for this book is available from the British Library.
13-digit ISBN: 978-1-7397705-4-9.
Design and typesetting by Gary Silke.
Printed in the UK by Mixam.

Edited by
Gary Silke

INTRODUCTION

Welcome to the FOX Annual No 1, hopefully the first of many. It's a blend of old and new, some familiar stuff and other things that we didn't have room for in the regular fanzine. We hope you like it.

It would be pure folly to try and sum up the 2022/23 season to date and try and predict where it will go but, force of habit, here goes...

Two-nil up against Brentford in a sun-drenched first game of the season and all seems to be well in the King Power garden. But City concede two goals and suddenly things are crashing down around our ears. That pre-season stat about us being the last club in Europe to sign a player in the summer and Brendan Rodgers' comment about us 'not being the club we were' are echoing around ominously. There is a 4-2 loss at Arsenal and, more

damaging, a home defeat to Southampton. Another defeat at ten-man Chelsea follows and they take not only the points, but Wesley Fofana on deadline day. A horribly porous defence, whose defending of corners has become a national joke, has sprung another hole. A home defeat to a poor Manchester United is followed by a 5-2 thrashing at Brighton and 6-2 mullering at Spurs. We are bottom of the league and 2022/23 is making Frank McLintock's 1977/78 season look like a picnic in the Elysian Fields, with extra scotch eggs.

Then Forest come to the King Power and we give them a hugely enjoyable 4-0 tonking. It's difficult to know if we have turned a corner, as Forest are so unspeakably dreadful. As the song goes, "Forest get battered everywhere they go!" A 2-1 defeat at Bournemouth five days later hints not. But then a humble 0-0 draw at home suggests that Wout Faes, our £15m signing from Reims, and new coach Lars Knudsen are having a growing influence on our defence. More clean sheets follow in wins at home to Leeds and away at Wolves. Players are getting their act together all over the pitch. Danny Ward, previously the subject of Twitter ridicule, is now a brick wall. James Maddison is back to his best. Youri Tielemans has found his shooting boots with spectacular goals at Wolves and in a 2-0 win at Everton. Wout Faes' defence, for that is what it clearly is, have conceded one goal in five games and that was a Kevin De

Bruyne free-kick that you couldn't legislate for.

We are out of the relegation zone and could really do without the rude interruption of the hideous Qatar World Cup. Recent performances suggest we'll be fine if we can pick up where we left off, and it would be good if Top's refusal to pull the trigger on Brendan Rodgers pays off. Too many Premier League clubs are premature in sacking their managers. Sometimes the right man for the job is already in the job.

Enjoy the Annual

& Up the City!

The Editor.

GET WITH THE PROGRAMME
Saturday 14th February 1976
v Man Utd - FA Cup 5th Rnd

Front Cover - Jimmy Bloomfield and his boys. Magnificent. 15p.

Welcome - John Smith, Secretary
"I would like to quote from a recent Sunday Express article which told the story of the brutal murder of a London old age pensioner, Mrs Doris Livings. I found this a most depressing and frightening story, yet it was an article which contained a message not unconnected with one of football's major problems. The reporter refers to a 'permissive society' and says: "As a nation we have been pushed into the terrifying position where our defences against crime have been demolished in the cause of trying to redeem the irredeemable. That is why there are whole districts of London and the other great cities where decent people fear to walk alone at night. That is why hooligans are rampant on the terraces in the soccer ground."

I have long argued a similar point of view in relationship to football hooliganism. We are living in a society which not only tolerates but appears to encourage wild and violent behaviour and, as such, blame has been heaped on football when the problem is no more than a reflection of the breakdown in respect for people, property and the law. It is time for a national campaign in which to awaken people to their real responsibility and the means already in their grasp to deal with the villains and thugs. The kid glove approach, with its ineffective fines and suspended sentences, has failed miserably. Bad behaviour used to be a source of personal shame for those responsible and everyone should be working to restore the old code of standards."

Blimey John, it's only the programme!

Action - Big Bob Lee scoring against Bury in the 4th round IN COLOUR!
Colour action for the first time ever. Our jaws are dropped.

Ad - Goalden Wonder. Pun-tastic.

City Commerce - Stuart Crooks

'This afternoon brings an advance in standards when we include full colour on ten pages, including our first-ever colour advertisement which was placed by Major Sports, the well-known Leicester pioneers of garment transfers.

We are proud to lead the way in colour production *at the same price* and it was with great excitement that Mr Terry Shipman, the City Director in charge of promotions, joined yours truly to see the first colour sheet rolling off the press at Hemmings & Capey.

This afternoon we have the pleasure to welcome Weetabix as our Match Sponsors. This is the result of personal links between City officials and Martin George, the son of Tony George OBE, Chairman of Weetabix.' One day son, you'll be the City chairman.

Comment - Jimmy Bloomfield

"The news that a Leicester-based consortium had collected half a million pounds on the Pools prompted me to think that I'd never heard of a football manager who had won a fortune on the coupons. Most of us are a little shy of making forecasts because we know that the game is absolutely unpredictable. Apart from realising that you mark your selections with a cross, I wouldn't know how to fill in the rest of the entry. I leave the coupon to my wife Sue, and elder son David. They have a go every week and occasionally young Clive puts in his selections."

Mascot of the Day - 'Today's mascot is ten-year-old Matthew Phillips of 5 Middlefield Close, Hinckley. He attends Westfield Junior School and he's a really keen footballer, playing at centre-forward for the school team and as goalkeeper for the 9th Hinckley Cubs. His favourite player is Frank Worthington.' Good Lad!

City Album - FA Cup Memories

Keith Weller - *"Our 4-0 win at Luton was one of the best performances since I've been with Leicester. It was a day when we would have beaten anyone and the goals were just poetry. The gates were locked, the match was on TV and my goal was voted Goal of the Season. What could be better?"*

Manchester United - Tommy Doc's Red Devils: Lou Macari, Stewart Pearson, Martin Buchan, Brian Greenhoff, Gerry Daly, Alex Stepney. They're good, very good, but we can take them!

City Scene - Thank you to Brian Wright Sports, Rutland Street, for the Junior Fox Mascot's kit worn by today's mascot. And to AG Kemble, Leicester Road, Wigston for the records played at today's match.

City Statistics - City are 13th in Division One after 28 games. Top scorer is Bob Lee with 10 and the average gate is around 21,000.

Action Line-up -

City: Wallington, Whitworth, Rofe, Kember, Blockley, Woollett, Weller, Lee, Garland, Alderson, Worthington.

United: Stepney, Forsyth, Houston, Daly, Greenhoff, Buchan, Coppell, Macari, Pearson, McIlroy, Hill.

But what was the score?

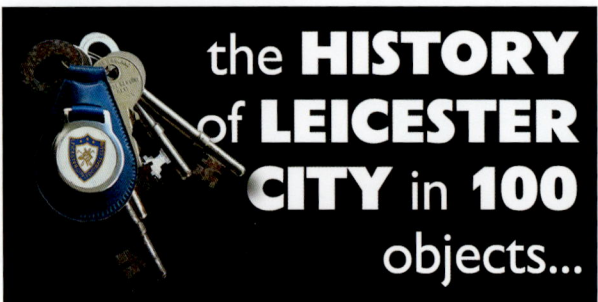

the HISTORY of LEICESTER CITY in 100 objects...

057 | boxing clever...

Andy Well explains the old ammo box proudly sitting on his lawn...

"Here's a few pics of the makeshift stool I used to take into Filbert Street in the late 1970s. My dad and I would stand in the family enclosure in the front the main stand from around 1977 onwards, with Frank McLintock's ill starred stint in charge being the first season I attended every home game. My dad converted an old ammunition box into a stool, which I decorated with players' names, so we could both stand behind the crash barrier half way up the shallow terrace. We would access the enclosure via the fabulous turnstile block on Filbert Street and try to get as close to the tunnel as possible. We'd use the box to carry a tartan Thermos flask and the half time Mars bars as well as a place to store the match day programme. Once or twice the 'ammo box' attracted attention from the police and we'd have to open it up to reveal its contents. It was great being able to see the match action from further back as a twelve year

old but my elevated vantage point was a bit unstable and I'd regularly fall off it whenever City scored. On one occasion we were perched directly behind a BBC outside broadcast camera but the eight goal thriller against Orient never made it onto *Match of the Day* due to a technical failure.

I also took along a homemade banner, which was stored in the 'ammo box' and unfurled, and then hung over the crash barrier. It was an old white sheet that I'd modified by cutting out the letters 'SUPER FOXES' from a piece of royal blue denim that I then sewed onto my home-made flag. Sadly this hasn't turned up and from memory I think I passed it on to my younger cousins."

058 | birch flogged...

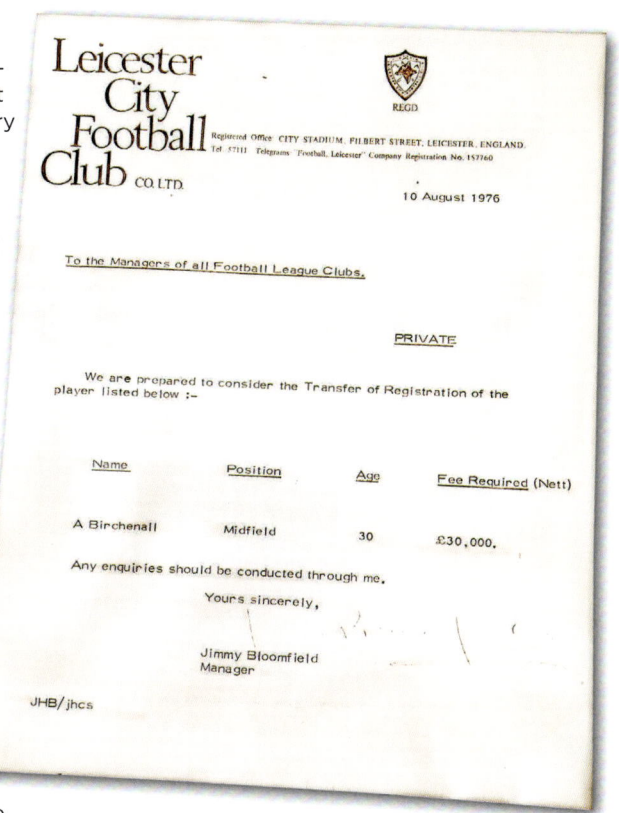

Thanks to Matthew Mann who sent us this ancient parchment from the desk of Jimmy Bloomfield. Jimmy had decided that a 30-year-old Alan Birchenall was surplus to requirements and offered him up to 'the Managers of all Football League Clubs.'
There were no takers at the time, although the Birch did spend the summer of 1977 at the San Jose Earthquakes. You can only imagine how much fun he had there. Birch actually outlasted Bloomfield at the club, moving to Notts County early in the ill-fated 1977/78 season. The dressing room could probably have done with some Birch-inspired laughs during that horrible campaign.

059 | grass in glass...

Thanks again to Matthew, who sent in this grass and mud ensemble removed from the King Power pitch at the end of the Premier League winning season. A piece of truly sacred turf, forever preserved in glass.

The Foxes Trust – on the ball for twenty years and counting

This first annual edition of The Fox coincides with the 20th anniversary of the formation of the Foxes Trust. We have been delighted to feature in every regular edition of The Fox since the Trust was first established. An opportunity, then, to look back over some key highlights of the Trust history to date.

Twenty years ago, City fans were worried about our club being wound up and having to be re-formed in a lower tier of non-league football. Following the launch meeting of the Trust, attended by over 700 fans in late October 2002, the founder members of the Trust and the working party spent many long hours over the winter months obtaining legal status as a not-for-profit organisation, encouraging fans to become members and raising over £100,000 to enable it to be part of the consortium that saved the club.

The Trust held meetings with both the Lineker and the Kinch consortiums. Despite the latter offering the Trust two Board positions without any investment, it was not convinced that the Kinch bid was viable, a view similarly held by the club's administrator. The Trust held a number of meetings with the administrator, with views exchanged as events unfolded. This was a key relationship at the time, although one that was rarely spoken about.

Many fans still to this day do not realise how close the club came to folding, with some of the initial consortium members providing funds to keep the club afloat ahead of the eventual takeover. The financial target set by the administrator was eventually reached, but only just. If the Trust hadn't raised £100k, the target would not have been met (the same could, of course, be said of any other consortium member who contributed to the same level).

The Trust continued to raise funds and, along with a number of fellow consortium members, it was able to invest more, raising its stake to £151,000 and in doing so it became the 14th largest shareholder.

Having reached the £100k target set by the consortium, the Trust had an observer voice in the LCFC boardroom, with Trust Board member Henry Doyle encouraged to contribute fully to discussions; the only thing he couldn't do was vote on decisions.

Away from the boardroom, the Trust worked hard on establishing various levels of fan dialogue with the club, from its presence in the directors lounge on home match days, which afforded the chance to lobby LCFC Board members, regular one-to-one conversations with Tim Davies, LCFC CEO and by establishing the Fans Consultative Committee, whose format followed a template created by the Trust. This ensured all fans' groups had permanent representation, with the rest of the Committee comprised of fans that sat in different parts of the ground, so issues affecting a wide fanbase could be raised.

During the early years, the chairman of LCFC changed several times, however, once Andrew Taylor took the position, the level of contact increased. Andrew quickly saw the benefit of regular dialogue, noted Henry's contribution in Board meetings and felt that the Trust should have permanent and full voting rights on the LCFC Board. Discussions went as far as this being written into the club's constitution, supported by conversations with other shareholders on the topic.

However, money was getting tight at the club again. With the team not making any inroads in the Championship, it looked likely that the best players would have to be sold at the end of 2006/07 season. Seeing an investment opportunity, Milan Mandaric launched a bid for the club.

It was very strange, and maybe very telling, that initially much of the dialogue was via a journalist, Paul Smith, who seemed shocked at the level of questions that the Trust wanted answers about. One such question concerned what would happen to the club if Milan was medically unable to run the club or if he, unfortunately, passed away while the club was under his ownership, as the

Trust were aware that none of his family had any interest in running football clubs. It was a question left unanswered.

Sadly, of course, four years ago, we faced exactly those circumstances with the loss of Khun Vichai in the helicopter crash, but we knew that Khun Top was fully committed to maintaining ownership.

There was much behind-the-scenes media work done by the Mandaric team during the takeover; this was not really known about by most fans. The LCFC Board were barred from commenting to the media while negotiations took place, yet Mr Mandaric, or his sources, frequently

fed information to the media. This included lobbying to the *Leicester Mercury* and its LCFC correspondent, Bill Anderson. One notable article there was headlined, rather ludicrously, "The consortium should give the club to Mr Mandaric for nothing".

Other goings-on include Mandaric 'disappearing' during the last two weeks of the January 2007 transfer window. Under the terms of the takeover process, no signings could be made without Mandaric's consent, so plans to strengthen the squad with a couple of signings were lost.

With the LCFC board unable to speak publicly, the Trust had frequent conversations with Andrew Taylor, enabling it to raise some searching questions via the media to re-address the total media imbalance. Having had many discussions,

it was certainly the case that many shareholders really did not want to sell to Mandaric, and the high attendance at a meeting at Grace Road showed a willingness to find an alternative option, however, a suitable alternative did not materialise.

So, one by one, shareholders started signing the paperwork to sell to Mandaric. The Trust held back until it knew the 75% threshold had been met, then signed its shares over before the level reached 90%, at which point the last 10% could be compulsorily purchased. It was clear that waiting until that point would not aid the dialogue desired with Mandaric once the deal was completed.

As we all know, the Mandaric era saw a ridiculous level of player turnover, and a revolving door of managers, two points raised with Paul Smith when questioning his ownership record.

Mandaric did, however, ultimately deliver on two fronts. One negative: he promised to get the club out of the Championship (we had our only season in League 1 … not really what was envisaged) and one real achievement: to sell to someone who could take the club further than he could. For this reason alone, we have to be grateful.

The Trust liked to offer support in other ways, including running a syndicate between 2004 and 2008 that sponsored one of the younger squad players each season. During that time it sponsored Richard Stearman, James Wesolowski, Chris O'Grady, Alan Sheehan, Joe Mattock, Eric Odhiambo and Ashley Chambers, many of whom made their first team debuts while being Trust-sponsored.

Between 2007 and 2010, the Trust ran a Schools Literacy project with pupils from those schools taking part being invited for a stadium tour, attending a match and then writing about their experiences. The schools worked with were: Townlands CE Primary from Earl Shilton, Forest Lodge, New Parks, Houghton on the Hill Primary School and Millfield School, Braunstone. The Trust ended the scheme after 2010 as the Leicester City in the Community continued the great work in reaching the vast majority of schools.

During the same period the Trust sponsored sports coverage on *Takeover Radio*, a community station run by young people for young people.

The aim of the sponsorship was to attract the next generation of fans, whilst aiding *Takeover* to get access to live reporting from home games, with Trust board members often contributing to the coverage. The aim of the station was to develop broadcasters of the future, with many going on to have long careers in the industry, including Andy May and Chris Siddall who both worked for Sky Sports.

Ensuring the club has a financially robust future is paramount. The Trust also aims to see that our club's heritage is maintained. The initial focus was how the old Filbert Street home would be redeveloped, and that recognition of the club's history was maintained on the site. With the help of the *Leicester Mercury* and working closely with the local council, the Trust, via a fans' vote, managed to get the newly constructed road named, and so Lineker Road was duly opened by Gary himself.

The Trust then worked to make sure the new (and current) ground was protected with its designation as an Asset of Community Value in 2013, meaning the Trust must be consulted if there are any plans to change the ground ownership.

Having a presence in the media has been the responsibility of a small team of Trust Board members since formation, with many contacts made and maintained throughout the years. However, two significant events, of very different natures, took our media involvement to new levels. The Premier League title win in 2015/16 saw the club swamped with media requests from around the world. The Trust agreed with the club that any requests for fan interviews could be directed its way. The Trust's media team rapidly had to be boosted by the majority of the Board, as requests kept coming at a fast rate, resulting in a team of 20 members fielding interviews. During that time, spanning several months, only on one occasion was there failure to fulfil a request (due to short-notice) and it became apparent that the Trust had assembled a larger team to handle the media than the club.

Of course, it was great fun for all involved, to talk about 'the amazing Leicester City story'. Sadly, a few years later an expanded media team had to be formulated again, but this time to deal with the media concerning the devastating and tragic loss of our club's Chairman Khun Vichai and the four fellow occupants in the helicopter crash at the King Power Stadium. Trust representatives did their best to convey to the world's media that the grief being shown was out of respect for the Chairman's character, his attitude towards our fans and his influence on the club's community ethos, providing finances or resources to help local charities, both large and

small. This was more than just being about the money and achieving a title win. It was pleasing to note that the handling of the events was widely praised by other clubs and supporters' groups across the country.

Over the years, having relationships within the senior management of our club has been key. As the club ownership changes or a new CEO is appointed, the Trust has handled each change and worked to keep dialogue open and ensure members' and other fans' views are communicated to those that run the club.

In the early years, as a shareholder, dialogue was relatively easy to achieve, during the Mandaric era it became more challenging but meetings were maintained with all the CEOs during that time. Under the current ownership the Trust has held a number of meetings with Susan Whelan. In recent years responsibility for fan relationships has come under the remit of the club's Communications Director, Anthony Herlihy. However, this is largely based on a good, personal working relationship with the Trust Chair, Ian Bason, and not an established system of formal dialogue that could be maintained, no matter what the club's management structure.

Nevertheless, this frequent dialogue has been beneficial, with a variety of issues aired, discussed and the fans' point-of-view listened to. The Trust is also afforded the opportunity to examine the club's annual accounts prior to publication and to raise queries at a meeting with Finance Director, Simon Capper.

The Trust aims to engage and work with all other LCFC fans groups. A recent example of this concerns digital ticketing, where the Trust, Union FS and the Disabled Supporters Association all aired concerns with the club about the move away from physical tickets.

Since the current owners took over the club, there have occasionally been queries raised as to why the Trust is necessary – after all the club appears to be well managed, we won the League and the FA Cup and all is rosy in Leicester City's garden. It is important to remember, witnessed by the recent folding of clubs and financial irregularities elsewhere in football, that any club is only one bad owner away from going to the wall. That is why the Trust undertakes to monitor the stability of the club now and for the future.

Good governance in football is a key concern of recent times, although it remains sadly lacking at many clubs. To this end, the Trust is run on open democratic principles, with Board members elected or re-elected at the AGM – this structure gives the Trust legitimacy when dealing with national bodies and broaching negotiations with various executives in football. However, the Trust AGM has also provided members with an array of guest speakers including managers Craig Levein, Dave Bassett, Rob Kelly and Micky Adams; several *Radio Leicester* sports presenters; a number of LCFC CEOs; Premier League referee Kevin Friend; ex-players Alan Birchenall, Wes Morgan and Steve Walsh. The person with the most roles whilst making a guest appearance was Chris Powell, who at the time was a current player, coach and chairman of the PFA. Last year saw the first hybrid AGM with attendance in person at the King Power stadium or via video conferencing, providing access to foxile members around the country. The guests were the then LCFC Women's manager Lydia Bedford and Emile Heskey.

The Trust is also involved in wider football issues, taking active participation in the work of Football Supporters Association (FSA). The events that led up to the six Premier League clubs withdrawing from the ill-fated European Super League indicated the importance of Trusts and fans' groups coming together to campaign for the benefit of all clubs and supporters in the football pyramid. Members of the Trust Board have played a role in the development of the response to the government's Fan-Led Review into football's governance. Going forward, we will be actively supporting the introduction of an Independent Regulator for football; the local consequences of which, may soon materialise in the form of a Fans' Advisory Board on which the Trust will want to play a key role.

The Trust Board has direct feedback on wider football issues from the FSA National Council via an elected Premier League Network Representative. The Trust also has representation on the FSA Broadcasting Working Group and the VAR Working Group. These posts mean that the Board has direct feedback from contact with executives at the Premier League, broadcasters and PGMOL (which oversees refereeing matters).

Football's attitudes to fans are changing and supporters are, after years of campaigning, finally getting a voice on issues that affect their clubs and them directly. Such issues include safe standing, supporter behaviour, broadcasting fixture changes, ticket pricing and supporter engagement.

Away from national issues and looking ahead locally, when the stadium expansion and wider development takes place, the Trust wants to ensure that access to the club's heritage is more widely available to all fans via a physical museum. This is included in the outline plan (a couple of locations are under consideration), but the Trust will work with the club in greater detail over the format and accessibility.

Join Us

The shape of football governance is changing and fans will have a key role in this. Foxes Trust will continue to represent all fans' interests, so come and join us. If you would like to know more then feel free to send your email address to Trust vice chairman Matt.Davis@foxestrust.com and he will arrange to have a sample newsletter sent to you together with an application form to join.

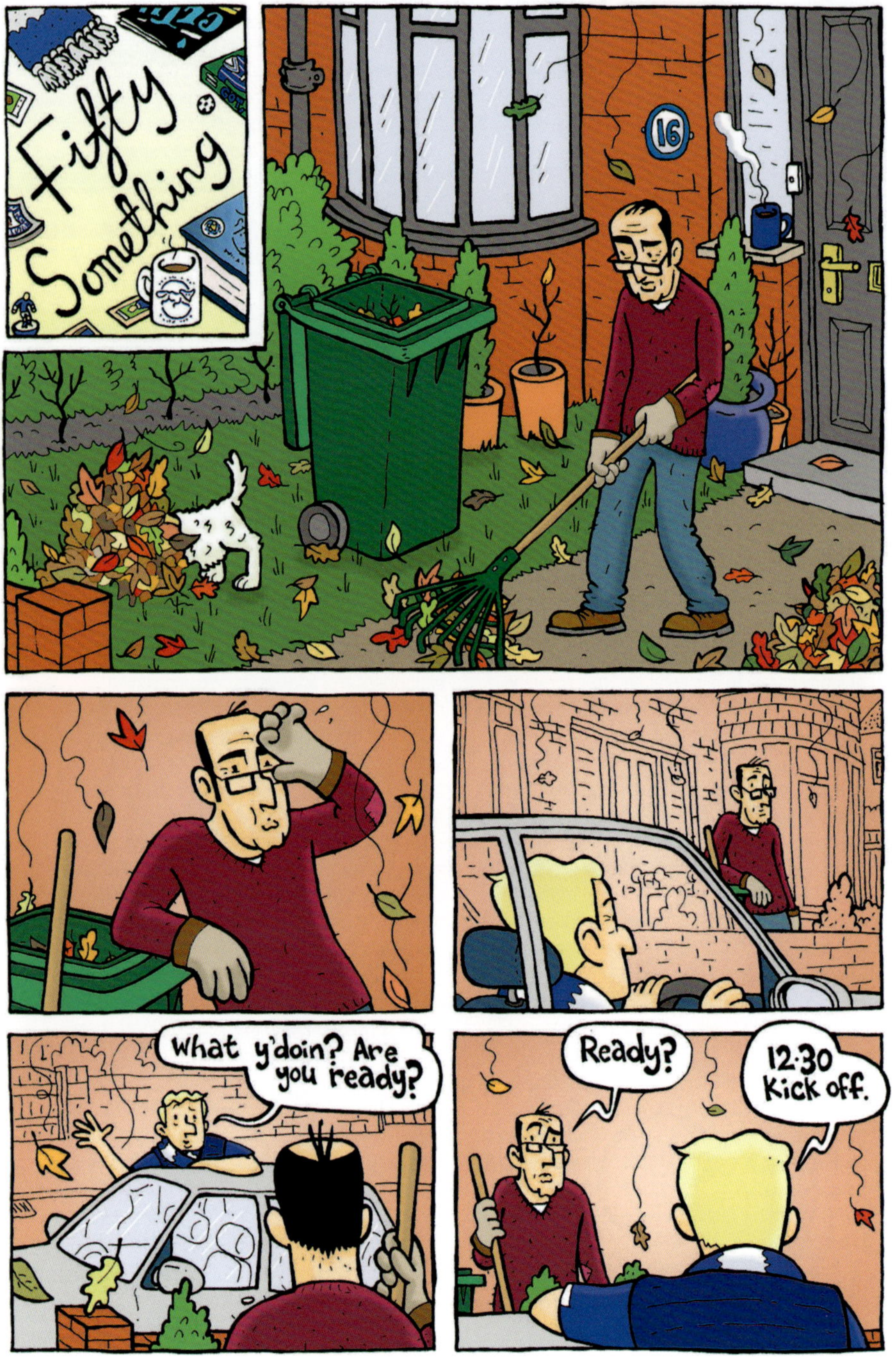

Despite varying degrees of commitment, we all agree that the team rules. It comes first, second and last. At its most extreme it can inspire the devotion to travel across the planet to places previously unheard of to spend ninety-odd minutes roaring on our chosen representatives. For that brief spell we are them and they are us. Few pastimes provoke that sort of loyalty.

But why? For those mentioned it is visceral; logic and rationality are not part of the thinking. But there are degrees within this self chosen straightjacket; one can tailor one's allegiance. A middling semi pro club in a small town can progress in the FA Cup to a point where its general population takes notice and *Match of the Day's* cameras lend cache to the area. Their normal attendance of perhaps two thousand swells to five figures as suddenly everybody wants a taste of the unexpected success. The inevitable failure sees a rapid return to the previous levels. But organised football as a spectator spectacle is seen as a proxy for community.

So there are the widely differing levels of support. The fanatical and the passing. But support there is, not rivalled by any other team sport. To begin to examine this phenomenon of comparatively recent human behaviour it means starting at where modern football came from.

Most sport lovers agree that we in Britain 'invented' football (and other games) as testament to our superior inventive abilities. We sing that football is coming home. In fact it is nothing of the sort. Its Britishness is coincidental, the origins are social, not national.

It is rooted in the Industrial Revolution when millions from the countryside

THE FOOTBALL FACTORY

beginning to gather in the towns and factories it spawned. Those enterprises engaged in fierce competition for their market share and their workers were encouraged to become part of that organised struggle at the expense of their individuality.

Team sports reflected the collectivisation and 'team' spirit necessary to the success of their firms. Unsurprisingly, the increasing formalisation of leisure activities began to reflect those factors necessary to production; a collective of different skills combining to produce an end product.

Workers, now becoming more collectively conscious, also combined in unions, clubs, societies and churches, all building blocks of the new communities emerging in society.

This formation of large social groups gave birth to territorial rivalry and the sporting 'clubs' with which we are familiar today were in effect firms organised by managers and coaches to function in ways familiar to those watching and participating. Many large companies incorporated sports clubs in their thinking.

There is some irony today that these clubs, formed as welcome relief from daily drudgery have, at professional level, now become more akin to those factories from which their forebears came. Owners appoint managers and employ staff who commit their loyalty and expertise to the enterprise which competes under an agreed framework of rules again mirroring the familiar.

grounds named after saints, and clubs whose nicknames reflect their origins from Hatters to Gunners and Blades.

So, today's loyalties sit firmly in the recent industrialised urban past. Leicester City is 'our' firm but it represents us on a much larger and more general way because social mobility has widened our scope of loyalty. Whether this process represents a cynical absorption of workers into the existing social system or innocent escapism is a long running political hot potato.

Unarguably the club stands for Leicester and its county. A symbiosis in which the success or otherwise of each tends to affect the whole. It is the only regular

Mr FRANK GARDNER President L.F.A and Founder of FOSSE F.C.

Today's clubs often offer hints of their heritage: PSV Eindhoven's origins in the Philips electronic giant; the Celtic/Rangers rivalry, the large number of demonstrable way to express our pride in the place of our birth, a pleasure not available to everyone.

Chris Lymn

THE CRYING GAMES

Men crying at football games, like crying in general, has become more normal, more accepted, even tolerated; not being told to man-up by mates or our nearest and dearest. My daughter recently scored a cracking equalising goal in her team's county cup final and I was in floods of tears as she picked up her Player of the Match award to go nicely with her cup winners medal. It prompted me to tally up all the times I have cried watching Leicester play. So here comes my own big six tear-jerkers.

Tottenham Hotspur - FA Cup Semi-final, Villa Park, 3 April, 1982
This game contained a lot of personal firsts. The first time we had reached a semi-final in my lifetime, first game not with my dad, first away game at the neutral Villa Park and therefore by far the biggest crowd I have ever witnessed, with 46,606 in attendance as Jock's Foxes took on the FA Cup holders.

The 81/82 cup run was a defining moment for many of us over 50 (admit it, back in the '70s and '80s you'd rather have won the cup than the league) and included the legendary quarter-final win over Shrewsbury. I will always remember the magical chant of "Wembley, Wembley!" that seemed to drift over the whole city as we walked back to our car.

My mate's uncle had painted his motor blue and white for our short drive on a sunny spring day from Earl Shilton down

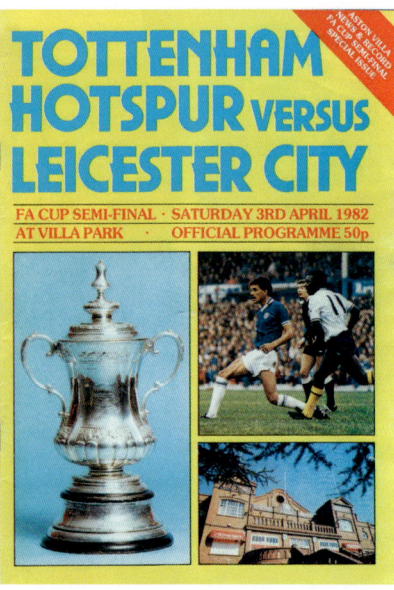

the M69 and M6 and a sea of scarves were hanging from car windows for our first FA Cup semi-final since 1974.

The Holte End seemed a never-ending landscape of faces and bare arms as we took our place in the stand that had been divided into two equal parts for each set of fans. Watching the game back on YouTube doesn't do justice to the hostility in the air on the day with Argentinian Ossie Ardiles being booed after war had started in the Falklands the day before. The two things that stick in my mind from the game was the magic of Ardiles; he appeared to glide, effortlessly over the pitch. The second was the Ian Wilson own goal that made it 2-0. From my blurred memory it was a glorious 40-yard pass back to Mark Wallington that sailed over the helpless keeper's head, but to my surprise, the video shows

Wilson, just outside the penalty area, chip Wallington, unchallenged.

When Tommy Williams broke his leg, it became all too clear that it wasn't our day.

My Manchester United-supporting brother had obviously been warned as there was no gloating when I got back home, weary and dejected. My parents needn't have worried as this 11-year-old cried himself to sleep as a magical day of firsts had been completely and utterly ruined.

Blackburn Rovers - Second Division Play-off Final, Wembley, 25 May, 1992.
This time, we went a step further and

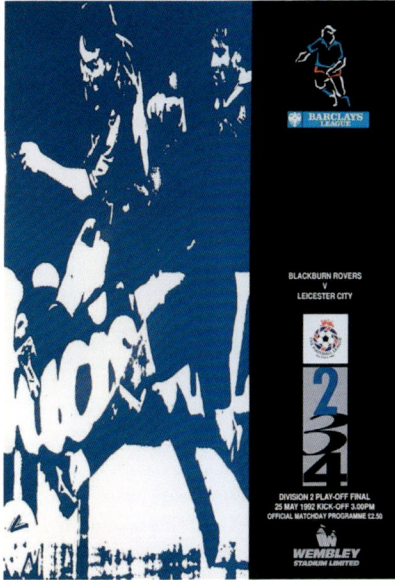

reached Wembley to play for a place in the inaugural Premier League season.

I'd travelled down from Hull where I was studying and met up with a group of City-supporting fans in Sheffield. We were in high spirits on the train as Leicester were on a roll, thrashing Cambridge 5-0 in the semi-final second leg. Brian

Little's team were very confident after a crucial 1-0 away win a few weeks before over Blackburn, a side awash with Jack Walker's money and with Kenny Dalglish as manager.

Of course, the penalty winner came as David Speedie dived over Steve Walsh's outstretched arm. City did have chances to equalise but it was to be no win at Wembley for the fifth time.

As I made my way to the exit I saw one of my Sheffield mates, Kev, who was red around the eyes and he set me off. I cried uncontrollably in his arms for a good few minutes before a sombre journey back up north. Speedie did eventually join City but was never truly accepted because of this, especially by me.

Sunderland - Premier League, Stadium of Light, 10 April, 2016
Okay, I wasn't actually at this game, but, being an eternally pessimistic City fan, it was the first time I actually believed

that Leicester City were going to win the Premier League. A sentence I never thought I would ever write and one that still gives me goosebumps now. Oh, and Jamie Vardy's brace also guaranteed us Champions League football the following season.

City, after a run of four one-nil wins, were taking on a relegation threatened Sunderland managed by serial fire fighter Sam Allardyce. It was probably my most nerve-wracking City game ever in a field that has plenty of competition.

An hour gone, still 0-0 with Kasper Schmeichel and the defence holding firm against a fervent Black Cats and a passionate crowd. Then, on 66 minutes Danny Drinkwater hit one of his instinctive high balls to Vardy who finished with aplomb. But hearts were in our mouths when Rodwell missed a sitter before Vardy sealed it in injury time. As the camera cut to Claudio Ranieri, he looked visibly moved as he wiped his nose and puffed out his chest. It was all too much and I excused myself to the bathroom to go and have a good cry myself.

Everton - Premier League, King Power Stadium, 7 May, 2016
The best day of my life. When else would you arrive at the ground seven hours before kick off? And pay £250 for a ticket from a Scouser off Twitter? Capping off a week that was more like an existential dream, as I wandered around in a daze, buying every single newspaper to check and re-check that we'd actually won it. Leicester City, my club, had actually, factually won the PREMIER LEAGUE!

I was hanging around the concourse chatting to anyone, where five days earlier I had jumped up and down on top of my car celebrating like champions do. I had the pleasure of a quick chat with Steve Walsh and then met Lee Jobber, the fan who bangs the drum at games. We were chatting about the amazing week we had just had and the emotion set me off. I'm sure Lee won't mind me saying this, but he's a big fella, and he just reached and pulled me towards him as I blubbed like a baby while hugging his ample frame.

Sevilla - Champions League, second round, King Power Stadium, 14 March, 2017
I simply couldn't believe we were there. By the end of the night City had joined a list of heavyweights of European football for the final eight of the biggest club competition on earth. It had been a weird season: poor in the Premier League but magnificent in Europe.

I'd had the privilege of being at all but one of our Champions League games but this was something else. The flags, the tifo, the fireworks, the music, the noise, the game, the goals, the result. I also had the honour of being sat next to my two young children.

Just before the half hour Wes Morgan

kneed the ball home at the far post from a free-kick and the King Power erupted.

Midway through the second half, Marc Albrighton's composed shot just inside the post put us ahead in the tie and there was mayhem all round the ground again. Although Sevilla went down to ten men when Nasri got a second yellow for touching foreheads with Jamie Vardy Sevilla finished strongly and a penalty save from Kasper Schmeichel prevented the tie from being squared.

On the final whistle we had a team hug and I completely lost it again.

Burnley - Premier League, King Power Stadium, 10 November, 2018

It's difficult to say what hasn't already been said about Khun Vichai and his leadership of the club, and how he made us believe that miracles can happen. But suffice to say he gave me the greatest days of my life and I'm so happy that his legacy lived on to see us lift the FA Cup at long last.

I can't remember anything about the 0-0 draw against Burnley, but I actually cried three times. The first time was on the phone to the ticket office. Credit to the guy on the other end, he told me it was okay, to take my time and it had been hard for everyone. Then I cried again when we watched the pre-match video-montage draped in our white scarves and again at the end when Khun Top led the players and managers past and present on a lap of the pitch.

When will watching City make me cry again? When my daughter makes her debut for the women's team or my son

becomes Jamie Vardy's successor? I don't know but I'm not about to get off this roller-coaster ride of emotion which is supporting Leicester City.

Rob Coe

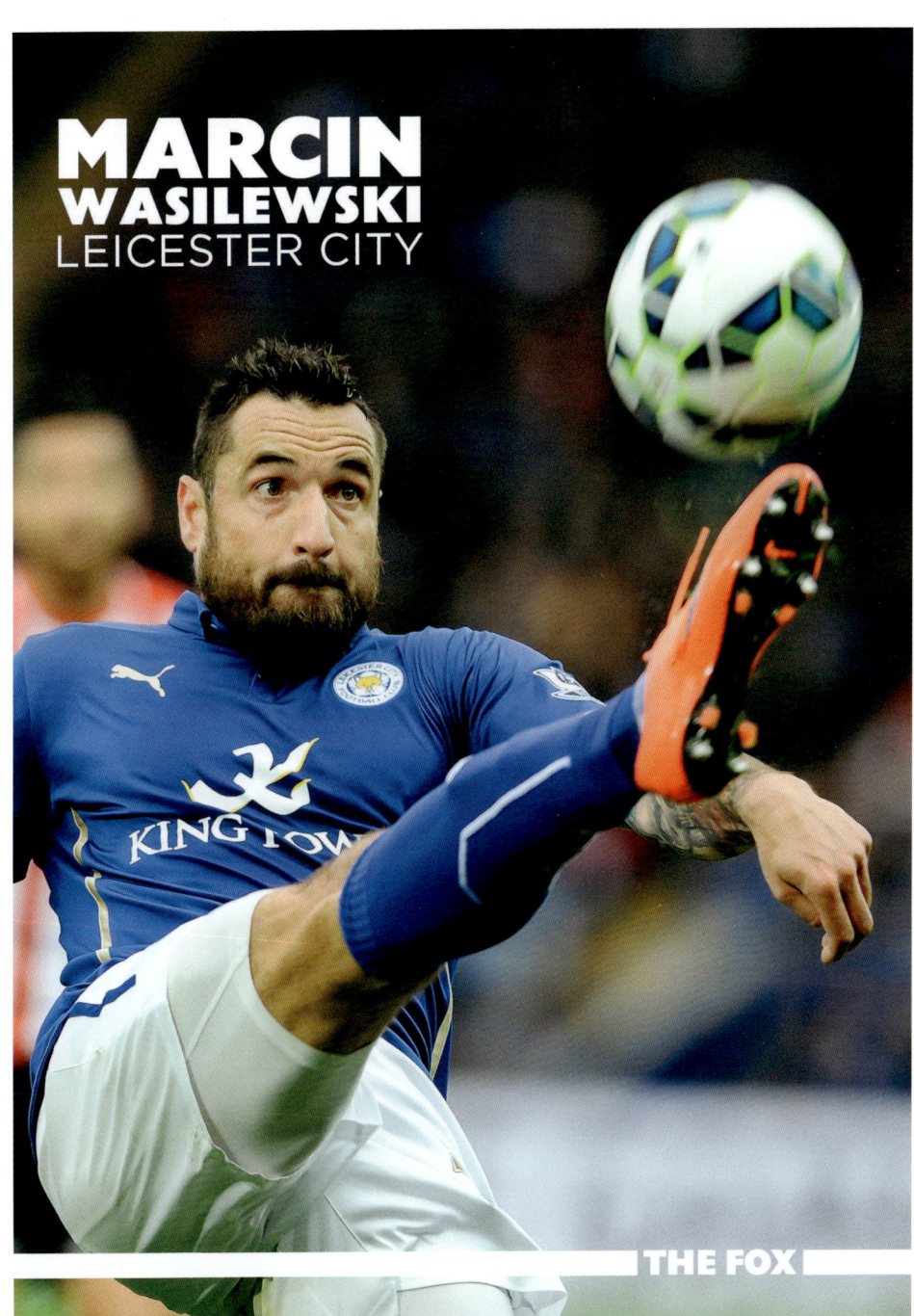

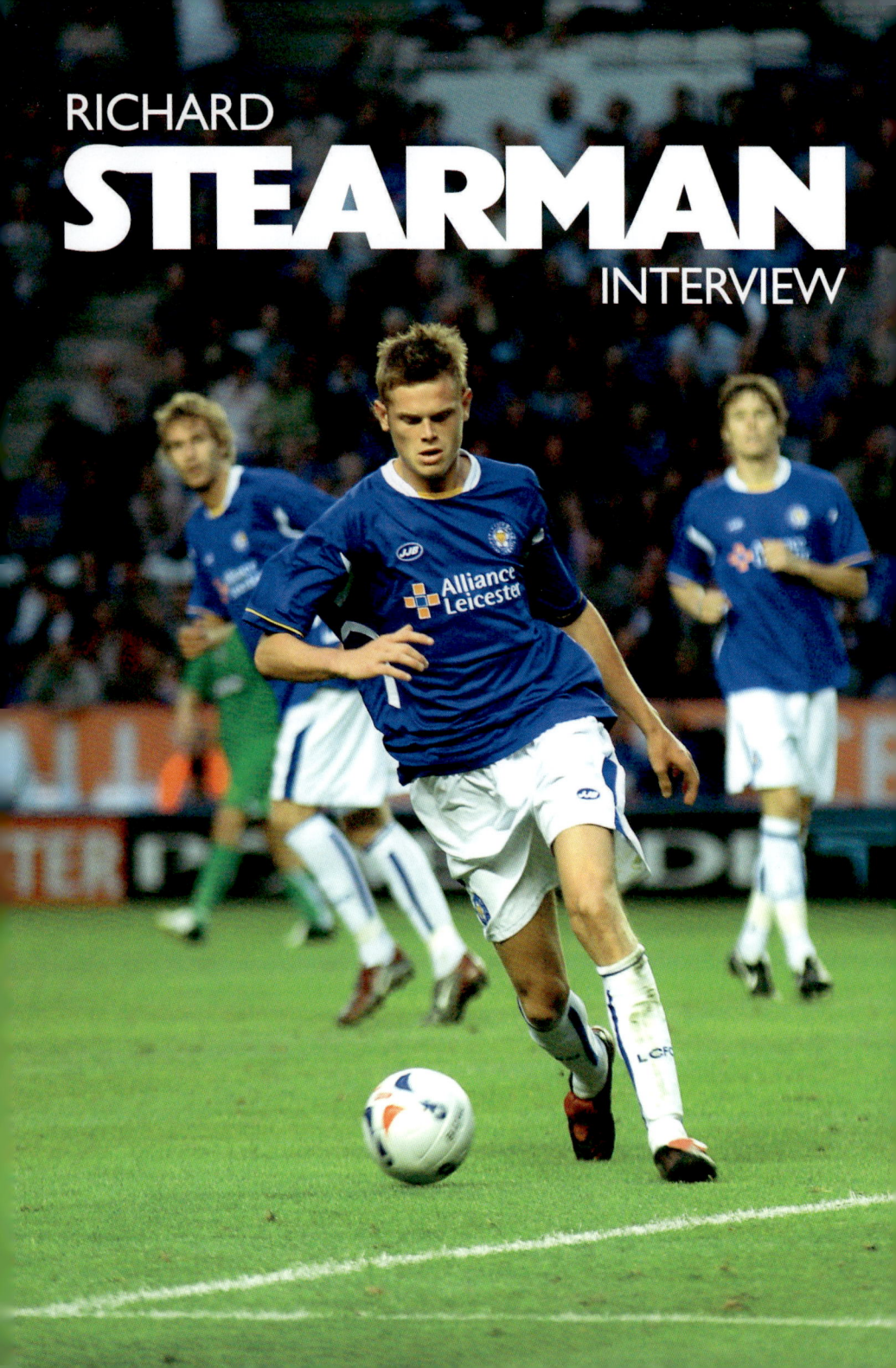

The Fox took a trip to Derby County's training ground to catch up with former City defender Richard Stearman...

FOX: Who did you support as a kid?
RS: Well, I suppose I should say Leicester. My old man was a Manchester United fan, so I sort of went with that. But when I started playing for Leicester at 10 years old I started going to games, sometimes did ballboy duty, and got really into Leicester after that. When I got a bit older I felt I should go with my roots a bit, born in Wolverhampton, so I also supported Wolves. But Leicester were my main team.

FOX: How old were you when you moved to Leicester?
RS: We moved to Market Harborough from Wolverhampton when I was four, because of my dad's work. He worked for Banks's Brewery and branched out to Leicestershire to look after that area. Market Harborough was where my footballing journey started. I was playing for Harborough Town and the school when I got picked up by Leicester.

FOX: How did you get noticed?
RS: I was very lucky, my teacher at St Joseph's Primary School, Mr Sexton, was very much involved in Football in the Community. A couple of his lads had played for Leicester so he was a good way in, and I was pushed towards the Centre of Excellence. The Academy system was only just starting then, I think my year group were the first intake.
So the Centre of Excellence was the best young lads in my district. Then we went to the next one which was the best players in Leicester and Leicestershire.

I got picked out for a six week trial with Leicester and then got signed up.

FOX: Was there a moment when you realised you were good enough to play professional football?
RS: It's many a boys' dream, and girls now too, to go down that route. I knew I had ability because I was getting pushed to progress. It probably wasn't until I was at Leicester City and under that umbrella that I realised it could be

 *I felt I should go with my roots a bit, born in Wolverhampton, so I also supported Wolves. But Leicester were my main team.*

a serious career option for me. Then you have to do the best you can and my family pushed me down the path of achieving that dream.

FOX: Can you remember your debut for City?
RS: I certainly can, Cardiff away, I came on for 10 minutes, centre-midfield. 2004, it was before Cardiff moved, at

the old Ninian Park. It was Howard Wilkinson who gave me my debut. He turned to me and said: "Stears, can you play centre-mid?" I said, "Yes, I'll play anywhere to make my debut."
He said, "Right, you're going on."
At that time there were only five subs on the bench, so just to be named a sub was a big achievement for me, never mind playing. I was delighted to get on, so young and competing in men's football.

> *A corner kick came over and flicked on to me and I was as free as a bird to half-volley it into the net. I wheeled off celebrating. A great memory.*

FOX: Your first goal came in that 2004/05 season...
RS: Yes, at home against Millwall, I remember it very well and also have a picture of it at home to remind me. A corner kick came over and flicked on to me and I was as free as a bird to half-volley it into the net. I wheeled off celebrating. A great memory.

FOX: You were only 17 when you made your breakthrough into the first team. Did the senior pros give you any guidance?
RS: Very much so, I was lucky with the senior pros I had around me. It meant so much when they spoke to me and offered some guidance and that was something I have carried with me now I am one of the older players. We had some very experienced central defenders at that time. I got good bits of advice, they'd take me for extra sessions. Matt Elliott was very good, I think he was finishing his time at the club just as I broke through. He helped me massively and I have kept in touch with him over the years. Others who helped me were Martin Keown, Dion Dublin and Matt Heath. They all looked after me as I was coming through and helped with my personal development.

FOX: Micky Adams left the club just before you made your debut. What influence did he have on you?
RS: It was Micky who first got me involved with the first team, but then he left and Howard Wilkinson took over for a short time. It was Micky who dragged me out of the Academy system and then bumped me up the levels that were above me. He got me training with the first team and took me on the pre-season tour that year. I have a lot to thank him for. Although he didn't actually give me my debut he was the one that thrust me into the first team environment.

FOX: Craig Levein arrived soon afterwards. Was he very different to

Micky Adams?
RS: Yes, I think what helped me was that Craig had been a centre-half. We had been relegated the previous season and we had a lot of senior pros in there who were trying to get us back up. The club didn't have the wealth that it would have in later years and they had to turn to the youth. My age group was pretty lucky in that sense, because we were needed, possibly sooner than we would have got in. It was a great time for us, almost being fast tracked, and Craig put his trust in a lot of us. He was forced to to a certain extent, but a lot of younger players played under Craig.

FOX: City had 'new manager bounce' a couple of times during that period, under Levein and then Rob Kelly. Why do you think that happens?
RS: Well, I probably got into double figures managers in my time at Leicester. A new manager will have a formation that he likes, players that he favours, so it is a clean slate for everyone really. A fresh pair of eyes might bring players who have been on the sidelines back in. You might have been miles out of the picture with a previous manager and suddenly you are back in. Everyone is trying to put their best foot forward trying to catch the eye of a new manager and everything gets a new lease of life. It lifts the pressure a bit.

I think Rob Kelly would be the first to tell you that he didn't really want to be a manager. He was a fantastic coach and a great person. But because it went so well

when he stepped in they had to give him the job really. That was great for him at the time.

His first game was at QPR. We won 3-2 and I scored and assisted in that game. It was a great night.

But being the number one was a bit outside of his comfort zone, he was happy doing his work on the grass. Helping, educating, coaching the players, he really was an outstanding coach. I think he is still in the game, he's had a very good career.

FOX: Early on in your Leicester career you were at full-back but then moved to centre-half. Which did you prefer?

RS: Centre-half, always a centre-half. That was my position all through the youth team, and for the England Youth Team. But because I was involved with the first team at such a young age, playing centre-half against 14-15 stone strikers was always going to be

> *Centre-half, always a centre-half. That was my position all through the Leicester youth team, and for the England Youth Team.*

a mismatch. I had the ability, but I wasn't big enough yet. So they got me involved and stuck me at right-back because I could run around as well. I think the thought process was that I'd be a bit more protected out there. And I enjoyed it, I could get up and down and had licence to get involved and score a few goals. But ultimately I wanted to be a centre-half and I left the club before I could stake a proper claim for that position.

FOX: Nigel Worthington came in towards the end of the season. 2007/08 started with Martin Allen. Did you find him as unorthodox as the rumours had it?

RS: I don't think anyone had played for him before, but we'd heard the stories. We knew it was going to be different and a bit exciting. One training session at Belvoir Drive we'd finished doing the warm-up and he called us in. We were going to play keep-ball, and usually there was an area coned off to play in but this time there wasn't. He got the ball, volleyed it high into the air and yelled, "PLAY!"
Someone shouted, "What are the rules?" He replied "Two touch, whole training ground."
If you remember Belvoir Drive it was all the pitches, these plateaus and steep bits, and the car park and we went all over the place.

FOX: Martin Allen only lasted four and a half games if you include the Forest match that was abandoned. Was that a bit of a shock?
RS: Yes, I remember that night well. I don't think I was involved. I was the spare man. You'd always have a spare man in case someone was ill, or got injured in the warm-up. And then Clive Clarke had a heart attack at half time and the game was off. I played in the rearranged game and scored the winner. Devastating as it was for Clive, it turned out well for me!

FOX: It was a strange time, with Milan Mandaric making sure everyone knew it was his club, bringing in players we're sure Martin Allen knew nothing about. Goalkeeper Jimmy 'Casino' Nielsen, who ended up making one appearance in a friendly?
RS: Yes, there were a few like that. Hossein Kaebi the Iranian lad was another. It was a strange time. Players were turning up who none of us knew who they were. But as a professional you have to be willing to give them a go and help them. A few worked out, a lot didn't, but I was just a young player trying to play as many games as I could.

FOX: With so many managers and so many players coming and and going, what was it like for you as a player? In quick succession there was Gary Megson, Gerry Taggart and Frank Burrows, and then Ian Holloway...
RS: It didn't help. There was no continuity or structure. You talk about the new manager bounce, but that doesn't last for long. You had some players who had already been here, some players of Martin Allen's, some of Ian Holloway and it was impossible to glue it all together. You really don't know whether you are coming or going and it was a tough time. I was just trying to

keep my head down and concentrate on my game, but it was hard on and off the pitch at that time.

FOX: It didn't end well, with the club's first ever relegation to the third tier. You played in that final game at Stoke, how did that feel?

RS: Stoke went up that day and the crowd invaded the pitch. I was just devastated. Relegation hadn't happened to me before. I was in tears as I made my way into the dressing room. I was upset that my club had gone down, but also I kind of knew what that meant for me. Potentially it meant that I would have to leave, which I really didn't want to do. It was a very hard time for me personally.

> *Stoke went up that day and the crowd invaded the pitch. I was just devastated. Relegation hadn't happened to me before.*

It was a very quiet dressing room, lads in tears. That's the reality of getting relegated.

FOX: You made a move to Wolves in the summer for £1.5m...

RS: Yes, Mick McCarthy signed me up. I think with add-ons it got to about £2.5m in the end. Leicester didn't have much money at the time so I knew I would be one of the assets that could be moved on for a decent sum. I was involved in the England set-up at the time and knew I'd have to be playing at Championship level to keep that progressing. I didn't want to leave Leicester, but the club wanted me out and I knew it would be better for my career. Unfortunately that's how it worked out in the end. But it worked out well, as Wolves got promoted the following season and so did Leicester.

FOX: You played under a lot of managers and coaches at Leicester and at your subsequent clubs, Wolves, Fulham, Sheffield United, Huddersfield and Derby. Which ones had the biggest influence on you?

RS: I think I would go all the way back to Steve Beaglehole at Leicester. He had a big influence on me in terms of how to be in a football environment, how to conduct myself, how to train properly. Everything that comes not just on the pitch but off it. He was massive for us as a youth team and a lot of players from my age group, and those that came after me, would say the same thing about Beags. Jon Rudkin and Trevor Peake were a big part of that as well. Manager-wise, Mick McCarthy for sure. He was a proper manager, a man manager and had control over everything at the club. Everything went through him. And he

helped me as a centre-half because that had been his position. He'd give you that tough love that you need sometimes, but also you could go for a pint with him after the game. A good all-round person, and I've had a couple like that during my career. Chris Wilder at Sheffield United, I had a bit of success with him. The old-school type of manager. I've also had managers who were great coaches like Wayne Rooney, here at Derby. Slaviša Jokanović was very good at Fulham.

FOX: Who were the players who gave you a tough time?

RS: When I was at Wolves, we were lucky enough to beat all the top teams, apart from Arsenal. For some reason Arsenal had our number. Their movement, everything about them. This was the time when they had Robin van Persie.

In terms of individuals, Luis Suárez was probably the best I've played against. Great movement, very hard to get close to, he was quick and tenacious and he'd leave one on you. Good at finishing, he had everything.

As a partnership I remember letting five in at Manchester City when they had Sergio Agüero and Carlos Tevez up front. That was a tough old afternoon.

FOX: Despite your England youth appearances you nearly played for Ireland?

RS: I tried and failed! My mother's side of the family are Irish, her maiden name was O'Malley.

Going through Leicester's Academy I went all the way up to the U21s with England. When I went to Wolves, Mick McCarthy had five or six Irish internationals there. As the conversation goes I told them that I was half Irish and they let the Ireland manager Giovanni Trapattoni know. He said to me, "Get your passport sorted and you'll be

involved."

I thought 'Great!' I used to go to Ireland every summer with my mum's family, so that would have been a great honour for me. But trying to get my Irish passport sorted was a nightmare. The logistics; you needed birth certificates, death certificates and all sorts of information. It took the best part of a year to get it over the line, by which time Trapattoni had moved on. I'd been on standby for a couple of squads but it never quite worked out. Martin O'Neill and Roy Keane got the job and they went down a different route. It didn't work out for me, not for the want of trying.

FOX: Your wedding made the front cover of Hello! magazine. How did that come about?
RS: Great question! My wife was a model prior to the three kids we have now. I'm a very fortunate man, probably punching a bit. She had contacts through her work so when we were getting married they got in touch.

> *I've got my A Licence and my Elite Youth Licence.*
> *I didn't want to get to the end of my playing career and not have a plan.*

Happy wife, happy life, so I did as I was told and ended up on the front cover.

FOX: What will you do when you retire?
RS: Coaching, hopefully. I've got my A Licence and my Elite Youth Licence. It was something I was conscious of, I didn't want to get to the end of my playing career and not have a plan. You never know how the back end of your career is going to go in any walk of life really and I didn't want to be scrambling about not knowing what I wanted to do. My wife was pregnant with her second child which was due in the summer, so we knew we weren't going to be going away. I wanted to do something productive with the close season so I got my coaching journey started. That was about six years ago. It is something I want to do, pass on my knowledge and hand the baton over. I'm quite a vocal player so hopefully I can cross that over into a coaching job.

FOX: How will you know when it is time to stop playing?
RS: My body will tell me. I'm 35 now and still getting out there and moving about okay. Once my body lets me know I'll bow out gracefully and go to the other side.

FOX: One career highlight to end on?
RS: Oooh. Can't really narrow it down to one. My debut for Leicester City. It was a very proud moment. In a way it was the conclusion of all the hard work and the sacrifices my family made to get me to

that point. I'm not saying I'd made after one first team appearance, but it was the achievement of what we had set out to do.
And the three promotions I was involved in with Wolves and Sheffield United. ◻

UNFORGETTABLES

There are few City players instantly recognisable just by the nickname. But Kevin 'Rooster' Russell is one. The bald-headed cult hero whose goals almost shot us to the inaugural Premier League season in 1992/93.

Let's get the nickname out of the way. The follically-challenged centre-forward actually acquired his nickname earlier on in his career because of his hairstyle, reportedly sporting a rather large quiff. Not, as many surmised not without good reason, because of his running style that at times resembled that of a cockerel charging across a farmyard.

His early career saw Russell released by Brighton before failing to make any impact at his hometown club Portsmouth. But things took off when he joined fourth division Wrexham. His 43 goals in 84 games caught the attention of City manager David Pleat who paid £175,000 to bring him to Leicester and second division football. But his career stalled again. 10 appearances for City in 1989/90 brought no goals and he was loaned out to Peterborough and then Cardiff. A car crash added to his persistent injury problems and it looked as though David Pleat had squandered his money.

Only after Pleat was sacked and replaced by Gordon Lee did Rooster come back into contention and then he became a vital component in two very contrasting but eventful seasons. The first is what is now known as the first Great Escape season. Russell played in all of the final 13 games of the 1991/92 season, scoring goals against Middlesbrough, Notts County, Brighton, West Brom and Portsmouth. It was Tony James who scored the only goal versus Oxford in the final game of the season, but Russell had played his part in narrowly avoiding relegation to the third tier for the first time in our history.

The following season was what truly cemented Russell into Leicester folklore. By then he was universally known as Rooster and, with strike partner and house-mate Tommy Wright, terrorised defences on both wings. They both scored in the 5-0 demolition of Cambridge in the Play-off Semi-final. Russell got the third goal on 59 minutes and I can safely say it was the only time I was still celebrating one goal when another went in, Wright netting within a minute.

Who can forget the goal he scored at Ewood Park as City beat money-bags Blackburn Rovers 1-0? The away fans were crammed in behind the goal and an unfamiliar red-clad City were attacking when substitute Russell was put though by Colin Hill. Mimms in the Blackburn goal came out of his area but his attempted clearance could only hit Russell's midriff, who then literally ran the ball into the empty net to a backdrop of increasing delirium. This put City into the automatic promotion places but the same Blackburn would come back to haunt us in the Play-off Final a month later.

Despite starting most games on the bench, Russell was in the form of his

life. Unfortunately he would never go on to recreate these exploits in a City shirt, being transferred at the end of the season to Stoke City where he now coaches their Under-18s.

A couple of days before the Blackburn game, City played a midweek game against Tranmere and a win was a must for the automatic promotion push. I was studying day-release at Leicester Poly and we had bunked off early but had to wait until very late in the game for Rooster to again take centre stage. Deep into injury time Russell ran on to a through ball from Steve Walsh and with his first touch slid the ball expertly just inside the near post at the Filbert Street end for a priceless 1-0 win. It had been a tense night until then, even Jim Rosenthal on commentary said Leicester fans had been "tearing their hair out" by that stage. But when Rooster did the business, the crowd went berserk. Legs, arms and bodies were everywhere as Russell reeled off in celebration. He ran towards us in the Family Stand, and slid to his knees with bulging eyes and an expression of unbridled joy. I should know because as he slid towards us coming to a stop on the touchline, he was looking at me directly in the eye. Time stood still, the floodlights dimmed, the noise muffled but his eyes shone brightly. It was our shared moment of triumph. I celebrated a last minute winner at Filbert Street with the man of the moment. For this, Kevin 'Rooster' Russell will be forever Unforgettable.

REWIND

May 30th 1994 - Seventh time lucky. After four FA Cup Finals and two Play-Off Finals had ended in defeat for City beneath the Twin Towers, victory finally came against neighbours Derby County. Sweet.

Foxed in the Head

Trying to make sense of the world using a brain rammed to capacity with old Lestoh stuff...

In this episode... Poptastic Pen 2 Platters... Football Cards from an alternative reality... A miracle in the House of God... Executive Pig Pens

"Hello everyone..." as the Filbert Street p.a. announcer used to say while we were sat on the terraces of SK2, reading the programme, not for one moment regretting the fact we had turned up an hour and a half before kick off. Well, we had nothing better to do. Beer was still something that, occasionally sampled from Dad's tin of Watney's, tasted absolutely vile, so a pre-match pint wasn't an option. So where better to spend your time than Filbert Street? Our place of worship. Gazing across the green (and increasingly brown as the season wore on) sward to the orange seats and executive boxes. Look left to the towering Main Stand and its jumble sale colour scheme of seats, slowly filling up. Right to the East Stand, well that always looked a bit shit to be fair. And in a time when to hear your favourite records you either had to own them or wait for them to come on the radio, LCFC would play them for free, courtesy of AG Kemble of Leicester Road, Wigston. Inevitably, some of these hits of the day translated into terrace chants. Kent Glam Rockers Chicory Tip's cover of 'Son of My Father' became an ode to Frank Worthington. "Son of my father, changing, rearranging into someone new..." was panel beaten into "Ooooooooo... Franky Franky, Franky Franky Franky Franky Worthington!" And splendid it was too. Party favourite 'Oops Up Side Your Head' by The Gap Band lent itself well to "We hate Nottingham, said we hate Nottingham." Or on certain days of the calendar, "Boots up Tottenham's arse, said boots up Tottenham's arse." Anyway, before I fill this whole annual up with all the many terrace chants derived from marching bands, European folk songs and nursery rhymes this is what

Chicory Tip: You can get pills for that.

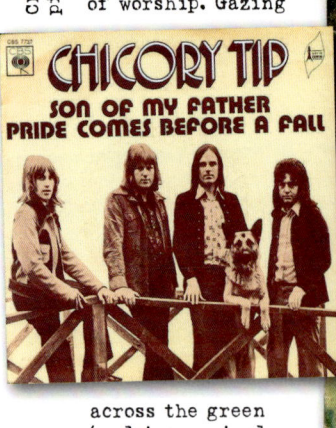

42

brought it to mind: it's great to see Kasabian restored as City pre-match music. Let's be honest, and with all due respeck to Showaddywaddy, Blab Happy, The Deep Freeze Mice, Gaye Bykers on Acid, Cornershop, Diesel Park West, Crazyhead, Yeah Yeah Noh, Ruth's Refrigerator, Prolapse and The Bomb Party, Lestoh hasn't been renowned for producing Premier League, world famous bands. But Kasabian are one, and 'Club Foot' is a storming track that makes the statement. 'You're in Leicester now, m'duck.'
Topped off with Jersey Budd's version of 'When You're Smiling' just before kick-off which gets the crowd singing, it has to be said that the club have got this just right. *

*   *   *

Hats off to Promatch who produced these cards in the late '90s. They appeared to have the refreshing idea of taking the piss out of usually feted Premier League players.
"I know, lets have one as a fat lad running for a bus. And an early '80s hairdresser. A man looking for a fight outside a bookies. An angry mother arguing over a parking space. A sex offender running away from the scene of the crime. They'll look great!"
Well done everyone.

*   *   *   *

Back in the '70s you had two choices of worship venue in Huncote. St James the Greater and the Huncote Methodist Church. We had no idea about the Protestant/Catholic thing back then. We just thought we went to the Methodist's because it was 200

Only Serge out of Kasabian could make foxes ears look cool.

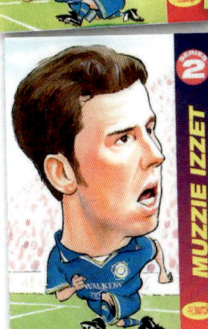

43

Going to the chapel and I'm gonna get stickers.

yards nearer our house. Sunday mornings would see me, Noz, Mitch and Steve crammed into the pews of a full church, uncomfortable in our Sunday Best, being bored witless by a seemingly endless sermon. If the vicar wasn't available then Mr Gladwell (who we called Mr Sadill, obviously) a usually mild-mannered, bespectacled chap with a classic combover, would give us some fire and brimstone, some old timey religion. Apparently, if we didn't behave then we would spend all eternity in the fiery pit of hell with Satan's goblins nibbling at our feet. The first few times we heard this it proper shit us up, but we soon realised that it was all a load of old tup. We hoped.

As I grew older I realised that Nature was my God and Charles Darwin was my Jesus. The earliest religions had got it right. If you want to see God, look out of the window. It's the Sun. It comes up every morning and provides our planet with the energy it needs for life. Not sure why the other religions had to be invented. Possibly law enforcement. In the Middle Ages it was quite easy to murder someone, what with no police or CCTV, but not so easy if you'd been told God was watching and you'd be going to hell for your crimes...

Sorry, I appear to have gone off on a tandem. The reason we attended the Sunday Service was that this qualified you to attend Monday Club. Which meant unlimited basketball, weak squash and Penguin biscuits in the church hall. We were the Harlem Globetrotters in three-star jumpers and baggy flares.

And here's the football bit. Once a year in the Methodist Church Hall they would hold a big fundraising jumble sale. My little brother and I perused the stalls, which were full of the most terrible tat imaginable... but wait. Amongst the old ladies hats, wooden gazelles, Top of the Pops (not the original artists) LPs, and chipped blue and white china, there stood the tall

imposing figure of Mr Spencer, the local newsagent, who had a stall. And, oh my goodness, he was selling FKS Soccer Stars albums at - get this - 5p an album and 10p a box of stickers. I nearly blacked out.

44

The Soccer Stars 78/79 Golden Collection was FKS's fight back against Panini. Throughout the late '60s and '70s they had ruled the roost, before Panini came along with their 'Football 78' album, with its fancy peel-off stickers and gold foil club badges. FKS had obviously noted that the kids would have stepped over their own grandmothers to get hold of the gold badges, so they produced an album where every sticker was gold. It didn't work, as Mr Spencer's unsold pile attested. We steamed into that stall and insisted that he take all our money, which was enough for two albums and three boxes of 100 packets of stickers. We immediately went home, tore open all three hundred packets and filled both albums. A process that usually took about six months, and a hell of a lot more than 40p. It was like living life at 100 mph. The only regret was that City had been relegated the year before, so they weren't included.
Recently on Ebay an empty sticker packet from this very rare collection sold for £8.50. I try not to think about the 300 that we gathered up in a big pile and yanged in the bin...

*   *   *   *

How I miss dear old Filbert Street, with its haphazard design, awkward corners and nooks and crannies.
My mate still insists to this day that right at the back of the corner where the Main Stand met the Double Decker, there was a mysterious gangway, lost in the shadows. I'm not sure about that, but more visible was a feature that I was recently reminded of while looking at YouTube.
In the summer of 1975 the club turned the Pop Side terracing into the all-seated East Stand. They had become obsessed with attracting fans who 'had a few bob' and after putting executive boxes where the Filbert Street End roof used to be their eye turned to the unlikely

Pop Side. It was to be all-seated, with a central section that "is the most sophisticated of its kind ever supplied to an English Football League ground." According to the architects drawing all you had to do was click your fingers and a waiter would come running down the steps with a tray of Worthington E and a Babycham.
Me mate Steve immediately took agin the idea and branded this new development 'The Pig Pens'. And 'The Pig Pens' they were, until they were removed a few seasons later.

Social divide: a lighter shade of brown.

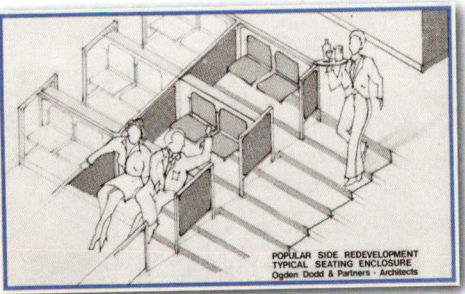

POPULAR SIDE REDEVELOPMENT
TYPICAL SEATING ENCLOSURE
Ogden Dodd & Partners · Architects

Although he did go on about them a lot and protesteth a bit too much. I think he secretly would have loved to have had a two seat enclosure and limitless dandelion & burdock. Rather than freezing our arses off on the front wall of the Kop.

* I have almost forgiven them for replacing 'The Post Horn Gallop' with House of Pain's 'Jump Around' for the first game at the Walkers Stadium. Almost.

45

THE GREAT KIT COMPETITION OF 1994

Way back in February 1994, in issue No 40 of The FOX, we gave you a blank canvas and challenged you to design a new City kit for the 1994/95

season. We had a huge number of designs sent in, some wonderful, some weird, but we loved them all. The winning entry was sent to the club for consideration, and was better than the one that City actually ended up with. Here we present but a fraction of what we received...

Jenny Blackwell, aged 12 *(right)*. We're not sure the world was ready for Jenny's experimental style, but give it another thirty years and this pair of designs would look quite subdued.

William Walton *(facing page, top left)* goes big on details with a nice lace-up collar,

thoughtfully placed stripes and a massive foxes head, introducing a controversial lime green for the away strip. His brother Phill *(top right)* goes for a more traditional look, bringing back the old shield shape badge. A solid effort from the Waltons.

I D Smith of Corby had two stabs at it *(centre left and right)*: "Please find enclosed two magnificent designs for a new City kit. When you have stopped laughing and picked them out of the waste bin give them a second look. The home shirt with the white sash and away kit of orange and grey is my first choice. There is a touch of Brazilian in those designs which with any luck will inspire the team to play in the style of Vasco da Gama or Sao Paulo. I know the stripes don't look

right on Big O as my mum always told me that tall men shouldn't wear stripes."

The very next season Chelsea turned out in an Umbro designed 'graphite and tangerine' strip. COINCIDENCE? Probably.

Thomas Martin of Beaumont Leys also had two attempts, with pleasing 'L for Leicester' design, an 'Ajax' which suits Speedie rather well and a sash. Everyone loves a sash.

B Whittaker of Wigston *(right)* has gone full-on candy stripes. A look later adopted by Asics for Villa and Blackburn.

Richard Jones, from Nottingham *(below,)*, abandoned our template to produce this rather graphically splendid effort that he "...would willingly pay £50 for."

D Rollinson *(right)* has a vibrant striped theme and adds: "Steve Bruce liked this kit so much that he joined City and tore up his Man United contract."

Also on a United theme Sylvia Mitchell *(right)* says: "We need to get back to having a collar, just in case we sign Eric Cantona."

Ryan Darlaston from Birstall *(bottom left and right)* introduces green as a third colour and Sampdoria-style chest bands to his 'mini-kit' design.

The kids are alright... Ben Brierley aged 10 *(right)* and Anna Rayner aged 9 *(far right)* let loose with the felt tips. Halved shorts may have seemed like the stuff of science fiction at the time, but City adopted them just a year later with their jade and navy strip.

We now enter the winners' enclosure. Darren Kimberley *(left)* and WP Henton *(bottom left)* both produced similar classy designs, so we amalgamated them into a final design (below) which we sent off to the club.

Obviously it was roundly ignored - they'd probably already decided on the new kits months before - but we had a lot of fun.

KASPER

As a City fan, have you ever suffered such a whirling conflict of emotions as the moment, toward the end of last season, when it suddenly became clear that Kasper Schmeichel was failing? Falling short. Letting the side down. It had to happen at some point. And now Kasper's seemingly eternal role as team captain, our ultimate professional, our club spokesman and undisputed leader, was finally almost over. Somehow, he was going to have to leave us behind.

I remember standing up in my seat and yelling at the huge, luminous figure blaming everyone else for the set-piece goal: "*Wake up, Schmeichel. Get off your ****ing line*." And I felt like a dirty traitor. A dozen angry faces turned and gave me daggers, though I was hardly casting the first stone. There had been whispers for ages. In their hearts, they all knew as well.

For eleven years, Kasper had literally been the first name on the teamsheet. One of my favourite City players of all time, and a worthy successor to our litany of great number ones.

If any single player has ever made a greater contribution to the history of Leicester City FC, no one springs to mind – and that just made it worse. It was impossible to see how this was going to end. Someone was going to have to bring up the subject of divorce with Mr Leicester City. Picture poor little Brendan thrust into the frontline on our behalf, to act as counsellor-*cum*-executioner: "Excuse me, sir, but you're on the bench on Saturday. Maybe you'd like to consider a move upstairs? To pack your bags?"

Meanwhile, no one in the club even had the balls to suggest that Kasper might like to try and learn to take four steps forward and catch a high ball floating into his six-yard box. Presumably, goalkeeping coach Mike Stowell had that very conversation every time there was a corner in training, but Schmeichel must simply have ignored his guidance. He was all powerful. Bigger than any mere coach, the manager, even the chairman.

Inevitably, this was going to get messy.

It had been almost ten years, a whole first-class career's length, since a question mark had appeared in anyone's mind against Kasper's name.

When Peter Schmeichel's son had first arrived at the King Power Stadium for the 2011/12 season, that's pretty much all he was noted for. In the previous season, City had gone through no less than five first-team goalies. What we really needed was a reliable Mark Wallington figure, someone who intended to stick around for more than 90 minutes.

Kasper didn't look like the ideal candidate. Having nominally been with Manchester City from 2006 to 2009, he'd actually been out on loan at far lesser clubs – Darlington, Bury, Falkirk, Cardiff and Cov. Signed up by his old boss Sven-Göran Eriksson during basement-league Notts County's fleeting dodgy cash bonanza, he proved a bit of a hero by later forgoing his mega salary. And so on to Leeds where the fans, predictably, didn't warm to the son of an all-time Manchester United legend.

Having been snapped up again by Sven, Kasper quickly established himself as first-choice keeper at Filbert Way. He looked solid enough. But alarm bells were set ringing when he was sent off needlessly at Forest, and again when he flattened a Blackpool forward with a homicidal challenge that, well, let's just say Mark Wallington would never have made.

Voted City's Player of the Year in his debut season, and into the Championship PFA Team of the Year the next, Schmeichel had steadily gained recognition as a very special shotstopper. Inevitably, having followed in his father's footsteps to win his first full international cap for Denmark, he began to be linked with bigger clubs – not just down to Mancunian nepotism but also on a global scale.

By the time of the Championship promotion season of 2013/14, it was clear we had a world-class goalie on our hands, and Kasper's stature kept on growing as his TV appearances grew more and more regular. He was well-spoken. Formidably focused. A born winner. A terrible loser.

Strangely, it was a routine League match against Yeovil Town that sticks in the mind as the moment when the fantastic prospect crossed the line on the way to becoming a legend. Trailing to the lowly yokels in injury time, Schmeichel came looking for a last-ditch equaliser in open play. What a fearsome sight, soon to become a way of life at City: Schmeichel possessed by absolute self-confidence and righteous determination. He always looked like he'd

get his head to any cross, by sheer force of will. Danny Drinkwater duly served up the ammo and… *boom*. Over the line. We all *know* he scored.

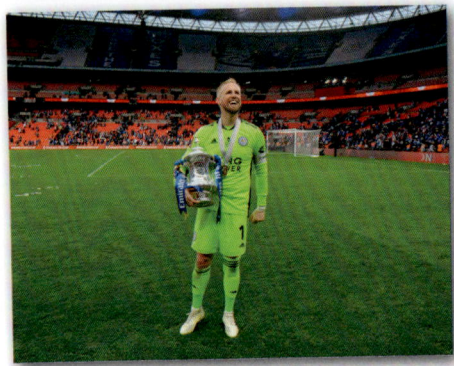

And then he didn't sign for Milan or Man U. He penned a four-year deal as we hit the Premier League bigtime. The love was 100% mutual.

Looking certs for an instant return to the Championship, we all know the stories of the 'group of senior pros' who locked Nigel Pearson out of the changing room and demanded more – *everything* – from underperforming teammates. In retrospect, we're not surprised that no one dared to countermand the irresistible force of Schmeichel & co. The Great Escape was ordained. Not an option. An order.

Of course, Kasper was one of the eternal heroes when Claudio Ranieri's Leicester City, impossibly, won the League title. You don't need us to remind you of your six-year-old child/rabbit/tattoo that embodies your gut-deep respect, admiration and undying love for the man. And then came those penalty saves when City stormed the Champions League the following season.

Maybe it was the sacking of Ranieri that raised the very first doubt about Kasper's unprecedented position of power at the club, again allegedly going off-road with a select bunch of influencers – 'the snakes', as the press branded them – to approach Vichai to recommend the unthinkable. The stab in the back, as vital as it may have been, was shocking. Unthinkable.

In the most tragic circumstances, any slight misgivings were then absolutely wiped out when Kasper Schmeichel was somehow among the first responders that awful night of the helicopter crash in October 2018 that saw our all-conquering Vichai perish along with four other souls. They say he saw the explosion, was embroiled in counselling for years afterwards at the horror of it all.

Nevertheless, Schmeichel naturally took on the role of chief mourner and club spokesman, as the statesmanlike but utterly empathetic voice of fans, teammates and colleagues alike. What a man. What a leader. What a debt of pride we all owe to him.

True, it is said that in 2019 City's coterie

of senior professionals then dispatched Claude Puel just as they had Claudio; but again any unworthy thoughts were banished from our minds as the hundreds of peerless match-winning, match-saving performances continued to mount up at City – and then the selfless, quick-thinking Schmeichel's reaction to stricken Denmark team-mate Christian Eriksson's collapse at the Euros last year. Teamwork. Togetherness. Love and respect.

So now I feel like a complete heel even mentioning Kasper's recent reticence in commanding his area. The unfathomable, sensational 'starfish' saves and full-length party pieces continued; but the high cross had, in truth, long been his Achilles' heel. And what of the hateful Slavia Prague, with their massive wind-up 'Foxhunting' banner and gutter-level references from the tinpot chairman to Kasper's corset, allegedly worn under his goalie top? Surely untrue. The bastards, making us even think about that possibility. And the same goes for OGC Nice with their classless slurs about 'the highest body/fat ratio ever seen in a professional footballer'.

Ultimately, what a relief it was when Kasper fell on his sword – perhaps sensing a tough season ahead, or a 1% waning of his magnificent powers – so generously giving Top an out, precluding the need for a stuttering, emotional dismissal.

For me, the final great image of Kasper remains him diving to stop Mason Mount's unstoppable shot in the FA Cup final, and the striker's look of complete disbelief. And then how Kasper took command and ran to fetch Top from the Royal Box. What a heart. What an uncommon display of understanding and empathy. What a friend to have on our side.

Without getting too tearful, does anyone else feel he might just be back one day?

Come back, Kasper. Any time you want. And this time we can give you an official role as coach or manager or director of football. All three, if you like. No petty quibbles here.

Derek Hammond

Get Shirty

Andy Wells, the author of 'Get Shirty - The Rise and Fall of Admiral Sportswear', explains how a global football kit phenomenon all started in a small factory in Wigston...

Certain old photographs can immediately transport one back to a particular time or place. Whether it be a family get-together, holiday... or the launch of a new set of football strips. The long hot summer of 1976 is commonly remembered for its record temperatures and water rationing, but to my mind it signals the year Leicester City finally announced a sponsorship deal with local manufacturers Cook & Hurst, and its trailblazing replica kit brand, Admiral Sports.

The Wigston firm had by then already signed up the 'Big Three' of Leeds United, England and Manchester United to one of its radical new arrangements, whereby the company paid football clubs for the privilege of producing and supplying their team wear. Up until then, professional and amateur teams alike had simply bought generic off-the-peg kits from sports retailers. But from the early '70s onwards, Admiral began to make individually designed sets of football strips for the clubs it sponsored. The firm's owner Bert Patrick, and his Managing Director John Griffin, hit on the idea that there may be money to be made from selling official replicas to young fans, identical to those kits worn by their heroes.

Incredible as it sounds, this groundbreaking initiative was considered a financially risky venture at the time, and it also proved hugely controversial, with Admiral denounced in Parliament for 'ripping off kids' by charging high prices. Not that this made the new 'designer' strips any less desirable to me and my school mates of course. The publicity shots from City's press day that

summer were considered as glamorous and alluring as any from a Hollywood red carpet event. Memorably featuring the perfectly tanned and coiffed Frank Worthington stood in front of the massive Double Decker stand. While manager Jimmy Bloomfield, dressed in a brightly coloured chevron tracksuit, looks every inch a jump-suit clad Evel Knievel, minus the stunt rider's bike and cape. The look was, quite simply, magnificent.

The accompanying publicity announcing the new kit's arrival included an advert that encapsulates this moment in time perfectly. The images feature a trio of young women with big hair, sometimes pouting towards camera, and occasionally in a state of undress: *Carry On Admiral*. The 'smudger'

Almost overnight, this small unknown hosiery firm from down the road, changed the game's appearance with a sprinkling of American inspired razzmatazz. Their unique strips became the perfect accompaniment to '70s football, which included a dazzlingly array of sashes, chevrons, yokes and stripes, accompanied by wing collars and logo taping, often in bright colours.

responsible for this glorious body of work was local photographer Neville Chadwick, whose studio was opposite Cook & Hurst's factory on Long Street in Wigston. "Bert asked me to organise it, and the club said, 'Right, you can do it tomorrow,' sort of style, on the pitch, with their new kit. But I needed models and I could only get two models at such short notice. So there was a girl who worked at Leicester City in the office, she stepped in to be the third model... and that was the result of the photocall," he told me, whilst handing over a monochrome print of a young woman with a blonde bob, seemingly caught by surprise putting on a pair of blue shorts. Advertising clearly works, as I did eventually buy the white shirt she's wearing.

For many supporters of a certain age, myself included, the name Admiral Sports still conjures up a golden age of soccer. *That Wizard of Oz* moment when our monochrome worlds suddenly appeared in glorious Technicolor, and the beautiful game received a strikingly bold makeover: Admiral's outrageous new kits looked like how David Bowie and Marc Bolan sounded.

At the height of its success, Admiral sponsored over 100 top clubs and international teams. And in the space of a few short years, its workforce had gone from making nuns' knickers to mixing with '70s football luminaries including managers Brian Clough, Bill Shankly and Tommy Docherty, as well as wily boardroom operators such as Doug Ellis and Jimmy Hill – not to mention showbiz celebrities Elton John and Eric Morecambe.

But by the end of the Seventies Britain was in the grip of an economic tailspin and chronic deindustrialisation, forcing countless local businesses to the wall. Which meant

that many textiles firms were no longer facing the prospect of riding out a recession so much as experiencing the death throes of British manufacturing. Within the industry there was a certain sense of inevitability that Admiral empire would eventually come crashing down following such a meteoric rise, with more than one ex-employee likening the firm to *The Mouse that Roared*.

By the following decade its contracts and roster of big clubs had all but disappeared, and the firm had "created a monster they couldn't feed" according to insiders. Adidas, Le Coq Sportif and Umbro had effectively taken over the replicas market, and Admiral wasn't able to take advantage of the growing demand for adult sizes. The company and its 400-odd workforce was also battling against the march of global trade, and when a nervous Midland Bank called in its overdraft, Admiral sadly went bust. Local businessman Peter Hockenhull stepped in and briefly revived the brand's fortunes – including a 'kit-astrophic' appearance at the 1982 World Cup finals – but it was to prove a last hurrah. And when the FA awarded its next kit contract to Umbro, the game was finally up.

It's the power and appetite for nostalgia that probably best explains why I ended up making a documentary about the firm's rise and fall in 2016, called *Get Shirty: how a small Midlands underwear firm changed football forever*. It told the tale of 'ordinary' people doing extraordinary things, and was very much a love letter to the place where I'd once lived, and some wonderful-looking football kits.

The ITV film proved hugely popular and had clearly resonated with other people, which in turn piqued my own interest

to dig a little deeper, knowing I'd only skimmed the surface of a far bigger story. I was also sitting on a wealth of recorded interviews, and I wanted to give full voice to these accounts, as only a fraction of the

chats I'd had with former bosses and ex-employees had made it into the final cut.

There was clearly scope to cover the story more fully in a book, and a global pandemic accompanied by a national lockdown, afforded me the time and space to start writing. While a call from a drama producer mate wanting to 'option' *Get Shirty*, and turn it into a feature film similar in vein to *Kinky Boots* and *Made in Dagenham*, gave me the impetus to finish it and find a publisher.

Yet without realising it from the very outset, delving into the past also became a

personal journey into my own childhood, as I unpacked a story intertwined with my own life, having lived close to the Wigston factory and being a part of the target demographic for those first itchy polyester jerseys. The book also became a story about Leicester's manufacturing heritage, a tribute to all of the people who worked at Cook & Hurst, and a celebration of what they achieved so brilliantly together – being part responsible for the mass popularisation of sportswear, later fusing into leisurewear.

Football historian John Devlin is in no doubt as to the firm's importance to the replica kits market today. "Essentially, it's one of the leading income generators for the big clubs around the world. So whenever you see a replica shirt, nine times out of ten you're thinking, 'That's come from an Admiral initiative way back 40 years ago'. The popularity of replica shirts today among supporters isn't waning, it's still there. They're still sold in the hundreds of thousands, and it's because of that Admiral legacy."

How big is the replica shirt industry today? Europe's elite clubs are each believed to shift around three million official jerseys every season, with Manchester United leading the way with an estimated 3.25 million sales. As for the financial worth of the industry, some claim the global sector, dominated by sportswear's world superpowers Adidas and Nike, to be worth around £2.5 billion.

The first kit contract Bert Patrick and John Griffin brokered with the Old Trafford club was worth £15,000 per annum, the same amount it took to sign up the England team in 1974. At the time of writing, it was reported that the Football Association had signed a contract with Nike up to 2030 that could be worth in excess of £400 million.

When I asked Bert about Admiral's impact on the sportswear world, he told me, "We were responsible for starting a multi-billion-pound industry. It wasn't there before, really, but that's what it grew to be. Admiral was the vehicle that moved off into the unknown, and it just developed from there. Because we had the vision, we were a team, and the world was our oyster."

So next time you're travelling past Wigston why not make a pilgrimage to Cook & Hurst's old Long Street factory? Admiral Sport's rise appears even more remarkable when you're stood in front of such a modest site. But this is where it all started: the cradle of replica-isation.

'Get Shirty - The Rise & Fall of Admiral Sportwear' by Andy Wells is available from Conker Editions, Amazon and all good book shops. £16

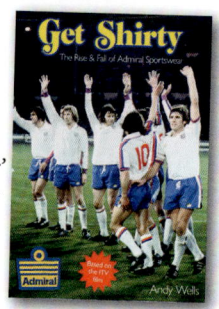

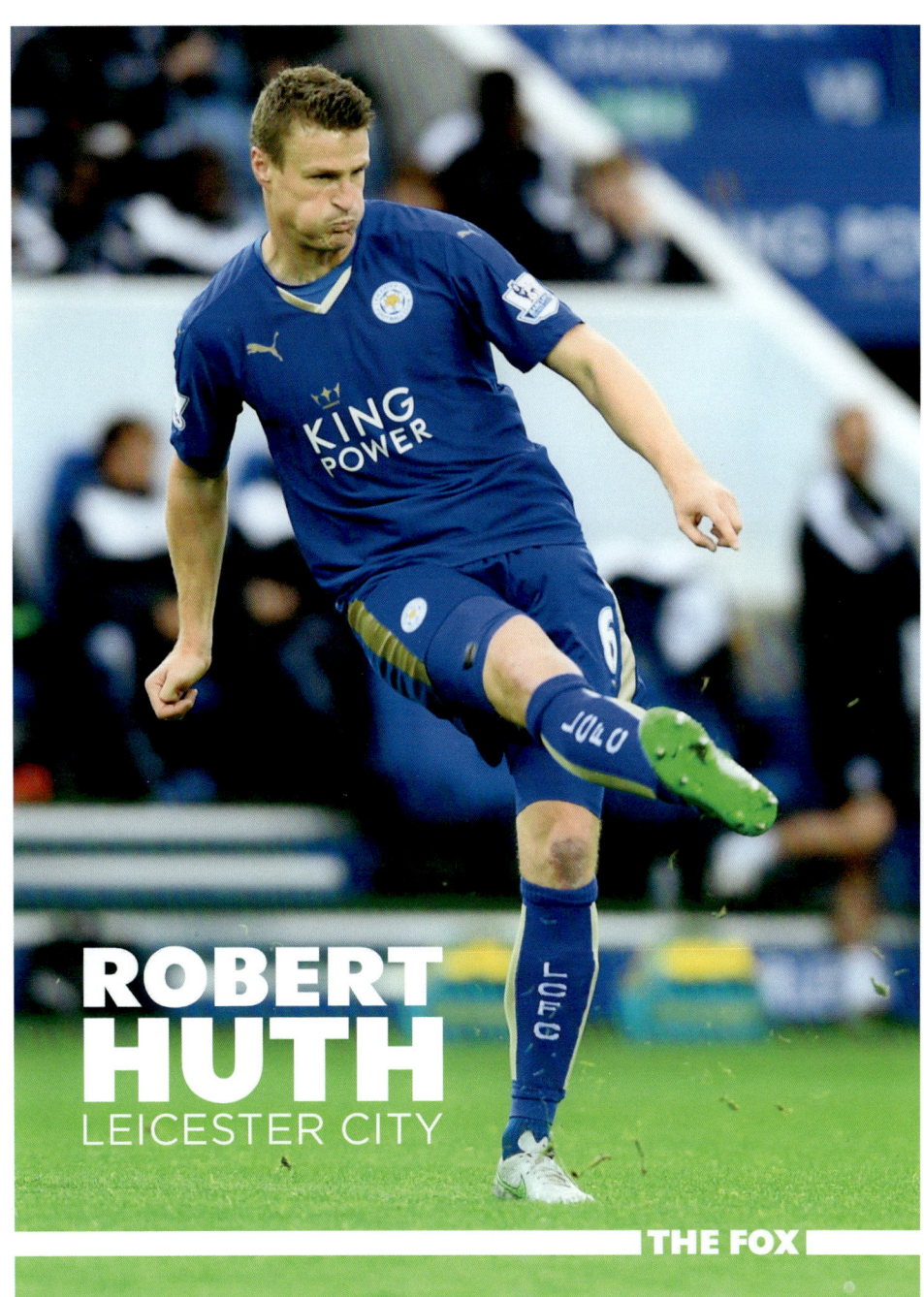

YANKEE DOODLE SANDY

Club Historian John Hutchinson uncovers the story of Alexander 'Sandy' Wood, a World Cup semi-finalist in 1930 and a Leicester City player between 1933 and 1936.

The first FIFA World Cup took place in Uruguay in 1930. Playing at left-back in the United States side which reached the semi-finals was a Scot called Alexander 'Sandy' Wood, who later went on to spend three seasons at Filbert Street between 1933 and 1936. This made him the first player associated with Leicester City to have played in the World Cup Finals. Along with Kasey Keller, he is one of only two Leicester City players to be admitted to the US National Soccer Hall of Fame. He was also one of the first of a long line of City players to have extensive playing experience abroad.

Sandy was born in Lochgelly, Fife in June 1907. In 1921, as a 13 year-old, he won a Scotland schoolboy international cap against Wales. Later that year Sandy emigrated with his family to the United States. They settled in a town called Gary in Illinois. Sandy attended the Emerson High School, before going to work for the local Union Dawn Steel Company and in 1922, he became an American citizen.

In the year that Sandy arrived in the USA, the American Soccer League (ASL) the country's first professional league, was formed. It operated primarily in the north-eastern States, with teams like Bethlehem Steel, Providence Clamdiggers and Brooklyn Wanderers at the fore.

In 1923, when he was 16, Sandy joined Chicago Bricklayers. Seven years later, by which time he was a well known soccer player, an article about Sandy in the *New York Evening Post* provides us with some background. It said that Wood claimed that his soccer ability was hereditary and that his father William played for Motherwell in 1905. The article also reveals a fact which, until this article was researched, was unknown to Leicester City Football Club. It states that his uncle was John Duncan "who played eight years for Raith Rovers in Scotland, then went to England to achieve international fame." The article doesn't mention that Johnny Duncan made his name as Leicester City's captain in the 1920s, skippering them to promotion to the top division in 1925 and to the runners-up spot in the top division in 1929, when his City team missed out on the League title by only one point.

The article additionally revealed that Sandy was an all-round sportsman who had "played in hundreds of basketball games, played golf and did a little swimming on the side" and that his 16-year-old sister Etta held the national swimming title for breaststroke.

In 1925, having opted for soccer as his main sport, Sandy signed a contract with Chicago Bricklayers. At the same time he began attending Northwestern University, later graduating as an accountant.

Chicago Bricklayers played in the Chicago Soccer League. During his time there, Sandy never missed a game, including Exhibition matches. In 1928, the team reached the US National Challenge Cup Final. This was the first truly national cup competition in the States. In the semi-final, they played Ben Miller FC of St Louis. The *St Louis Dispatch* at the time was full of praise for Sandy's side praising them as a very good, mainly Scottish side which had won 17 and drawn one of their 18 matches so far that season.

In the Final, played over two legs, the Bricklayers lost 3-1 on aggregate to the ASL side, the New York Nationals. The games were played at New York's Polo ground and at Chicago's Soldier Field in front of an aggregate crowd of 31,000.

The following year, in 1929, Sandy moved to Detroit to play for Holley Carburetors who had reached the National Challenge Cup Final in 1927. In March 1930, Sandy was in their team which was defeated by Bruell American-Hungarians of Cleveland in the semi-final of the National Challenge Cup.

It was whilst playing in Detroit that Sandy was asked to play for the United States team chosen for the inaugural FIFA World Cup scheduled to take place in Uruguay in 1930. This invitation followed a trial match in March 1930, at Starlight Park in New York. This game was between a USA team and the Hakoah All Stars and was part of the process of picking the final USA squad to compete in Uruguay. An account in the *St Louis Dispatch* at the time praised Sandy with the words, "Wood at full back was as safe as the US Treasury. He was always there when wanted and he kicked a nice length throughout".

Before 1930, the USA had only ever played 11 international games. Instead of a qualifying tournament, all of FIFA's 41 members were invited to participate. At this time, England, Wales, Scotland and Northern Ireland were not members of FIFA, having withdrawn in 1928. Because of the immense time it took to travel from Europe to South America in 1930, only four European teams – Belgium, France, Romania and Yugoslavia – accepted the invitation to participate. Mexico, USA, Argentina, Bolivia, Brazil, Chile, Paraguay, Peru and Uruguay also accepted. There should have been a fourteenth team, but the Egyptian team's ship from Africa was slowed down due to a storm in the Mediterranean

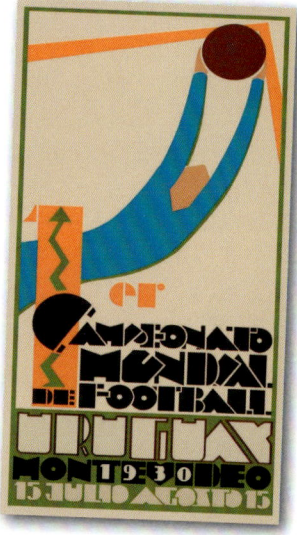

Sea and they missed their transatlantic connection.

The USA squad was strengthened by professionals from the ASL. It included six British-born players, but only one of them had played professionally in Britain. This was George Moorhouse, from Tranmere Rovers. The squad sailed to Uruguay on the S.S Munargo. They trained throughout the 18-day voyage. There was no alcohol on the ship and they couldn't train with a ball, but they did fitness work on the deck, played cards and had 'singalongs'. They arrived at Montevideo on 1st July, twelve days before their opening match.

Once all the teams had arrived in Uruguay, they were split into four groups for the first round. One group contained four teams, while the remaining three groups comprised three squads apiece. The USA were drawn into Group Four with Belgium and Paraguay.

There were two matches on the first day of the tournament. The second game saw the USA defeat Belgium 3-0 in front of a crowd of 15,000 at the Centenario Stadium in Montevideo. The pitch was described as 'a bed of wet, sticky clay with pools of water too numerous to count'.

The USA's second game was their final group match against Paraguay in front of a crowd of 20,000. This was another 3-0 victory, with the World Cup's first ever hattrick, scored by Bert Patenaude. This victory secured a place in the semi-finals.

By this time, Sandy's team had acquired the nickname, 'The Shotputters', because of their impressive bulk.

In the semi-final, played in front of an estimated 112,000 crowd at the Centenario Stadium, the USA team, with Sandy at left-back, lost 6-1 to Argentina. Just four minutes into the game goalkeeper James Douglas badly twisted his knee. Then defender Ralph Tracey broke his right leg, but continued until half time, with Argentina 1-0 ahead.

In the second half, Tracey was unable to continue and with no substitutions the USA team was reduced to ten men. Argentina took advantage and extended their lead to 6-0. Midfielder Jim Brown scored a consolation goal in the last minute. Brown later recalled that the Argentinians were brutal and 'kicked the USA off the park'.

The USA team was scheduled to play the other semi-final losers Yugoslavia in a third place consolation match prior to the final, but the Europeans refused to play. Consequently, the Americans were awarded third-place in the 1930 FIFA World Cup.

Sandy Wood was therefore the first player with Leicester City associations to be a World Cup semi-finalist. The others were Peter Shilton and Pontus Kaamark (both with other clubs at the time), together with Gordon Banks, Muzzy Izzet, Harry Maguire and Jamie Vardy who were all Leicester City players when they made their semi-final appearances.

In the final, Uruguay defeated Argentina 4-2 to become the first-ever World Cup champions. Before leaving Uruguay, Sandy's

Sandy decided to return to Britain. This is where Leicester City enters the story.

In 1932, City, (who had finished third in the Football League in 1928 and runners-up in 1929 under the captaincy of Sandy's uncle Johnny Duncan), was an ageing side which was beginning to struggle in the top flight. In March 1932, Peter Hodge, who had laid the foundations for City's success in the 1920s, returned to Filbert Street as secretary/manager. On 20th October 1932, an entry in the Director's Minutes book reads, "A letter was read from a friend of the Secretary's informing him that a left-back was coming home from America and if we were interested, he would help us to secure his services. It was resolved to leave it in the hands of the Secretary to try and come to terms for the player to come to us".

USA team played back-to-back games against Uruguayan teams Nacional and Penarol (losing both) before moving onto Brazil. There they played top Brazilian sides, drawing with Santos and losing to Sao Paulo and Botafogo. In addition, Sandy won his fourth and final USA cap when he was in the team which lost 4-3 to Brazil in the first international match between those two nations.

In November 1930, on his return to the United States, Sandy moved to New York, signing for Brooklyn Wanderers to play in the ASL. This was his first professional contract.

In his first season, his new team finished runners-up in the ASL. However the club then folded and the ASL itself disintegrated in the spring of 1933. Although it was re-established, it would never regain the success enjoyed by the first ASL. American soccer was entering into a bleak period after a period of success in the 1920s when the ASL had been second only to baseball as the most successful professional league in the USA. The main reason for soccer's difficulties at this time was the onset of the Depression following the Wall Street Crash in 1929. This led to a period of high unemployment and poverty. The bedrock of support on which soccer depended was eroded.

In 1932, after a two year break from the game, and finding it difficult to find work,

Leicester City Players photographed at the L.M.S. Station before entraining for Preston for to-morrow's cup-tie. Left to right: Adcock, Grosvenor, Laurie Edwards (trainer), Gardiner, Liddle, Jon es, Black, Lochhead, Chandler, Smith, Maw, McLaren, Heywood, and Wood.

The minutes make no reference whatsoever to the family connection between Sandy and Johnny Duncan, who had left the club in 1930 after the Directors had refused his request to become landlord of the Turks Head, a public house opposite the gates of Leicester prison.

Peter Hodge met Sandy on 26th October 1932 and the player intimated that he was willing to sign. However it was to be another four months before Sandy was able to sign for City. There was a hitch relating to the immigration regulations. In late November, Hodge and Wood went to the Home Office and to the Ministry of Labour to try to resolve this but to no avail. The issue remained unresolved until February 1933, when the Directors Minutes recorded, "The manager reported that the player had received a permit to stay in this country and he has been signed on." The minutes went on to record that the terms specified a £10 signing on fee and a weekly wage of £5, with an extra £1 if he was in the first team.

A month later, Sandy made his debut against Blackpool at Filbert Street with the club bottom of the table. He played in the remaining nine games of the season. City won five and drew two of these games. Still bottom of the table with only three games to go, the City won all three and finished 19th, avoiding relegation by two points.

The following season (1933/34) City struggled again. Competing with Welsh international full-back Dai Jones for a place in the first team, Sandy established himself as first choice in January 1934.

Later that season, Leicester reached the semi-final of the FA Cup for the first time in the club's history. Having played in the victories in the 4th and 5th rounds against Millwall and Birmingham City and in the quarter-final against Preston North End Sandy was selected for the FA Cup semi-final against Portsmouth. Their side contained two of the brothers of the Leicester star Sep Smith, who was on the verge of being selected for England. 66,544 fans watched the game at Birmingham City's St Andrews ground. Leicester lost 4-1. The headline in the *Leicester Mercury* report was, 'Bad Three Minutes and Wembley Slips Away'. The sub-heading 'Drama of City's Injured Player' referred to Sandy Wood who broke his nose just before half time after running into and falling over a touchline photographer. By this time, with a dazzling sun in the City players' eyes, Portsmouth were leading 2-1. Two more Pompey goals in the first five minutes of the second half sealed City's fate and Sandy was denied the chance of adding an FA Cup Final to his World Cup semi-final four years earlier. Sandy missed the last six games of the season after breaking his collar bone at Sheffield Wednesday with Leicester finishing 17th in the top flight.

During the close season, Peter Hodge unexpectedly died with stomach cancer and he was replaced as manager by Arthur Lochhead, one of the club's stars during the previous nine seasons.

The following season (1934/35) was the final one at Filbert Street for three of the ageing stars of the halcyon days of the 1920s. These were Adam Black, (who held the club record for most appearances), Arthur Chandler (the club's record goalscorer) and

England international winger Hugh Adcock. Sandy meanwhile re-established himself in the first team in December 1934 missing only four league games for the rest of the season which unfortunately ended in relegation after ten successive campaigns in the old First Division.

Sandy started the following season as first choice left-back but soon lost his place to Dai Jones who had been playing at right-back until the emergence of Billy Frame who made that position his own for several years to come.

At the end of the season Sandy was placed on the transfer list. The Directors' Minutes of 5th May 1936 record that he applied for his transfer fee of £750 to be reduced, but on 13th May he moved to Second Division Nottingham Forest for the full fee of £750. He stayed there for one season, making 22 appearances. The late Paul Taylor's research uncovered the fact that he suffered a bankruptcy hearing in Nottingham following betting losses which left him with a bank balance of £1.

Things picked up for Sandy the following season. In March 1937, a new professional club called Colchester United was formed. It entered the Southern League and appointed ex-Leicester player George Ritchie – a key member of the side which finished runners-up in 1929 – as its new skipper. Recreating the left flank combination they had at Filbert Street, Sandy and George Ritchie helped Colchester United to win the Southern League Cup at the end of their first season at Layer Road.

The following season (1938/39) Sandy joined Chelmsford City. This was another newly formed professional side about to embark on its inaugural season in the Southern League. During that season Sandy featured in Chelmsford's FA Cup run which saw it progress to the 4th round, having beaten the Football League sides Darlington and Southampton in the 2nd and 3rd rounds.

Whilst playing for Colchester United and Chelmsford City, Sandy found himself in opposition on at least eight occasions to his USA World Cup team mate Jim Brown, who after spells at Manchester United, Brentford, and Tottenham Hotspur between 1932 and 1937, was playing for Guildford City.

The Second World War broke out in September 1939. A month later, after a brief spell working in a Marconi Radio factory, Sandy returned to the USA. He went back to Gary where he worked for the US Steel Corporation until he retired in 1970 at the age of 63.

It is fitting, in this World Cup Year, that we remember Sandy Wood, the Leicester City player who played in the first ever World Cup, as well as in the American Soccer League. In England, he played in the English First and Second Divisions of the Football League and in the Southern League. It was these experiences which resulted in Sandy being inducted into the US Soccer Hall of Fame in 1986. A year later, Sandy died in Gary soon after his 80th birthday.

With thanks to Nathen McVittie, not only for his help with US soccer history, but also for putting me in contact with Jim Brown's grandson James Brown (Society of American Soccer History and the US National Soccer Hall of Fame) and US soccer Historian Chuck Nolan Jnr. Their knowledge and archive pictures were invaluable. Several of the photographs in this piece were provided by Sandy's grandson Bill Wood and his wife Avril. These pictures had belonged to Sandy's son the late William R Wood. One result of these contacts with the Wood family was that Bill and Avril were recently invited to King Power Stadium whilst they were on a visit to the UK from the USA.

DAVID KELLY INTERVIEW

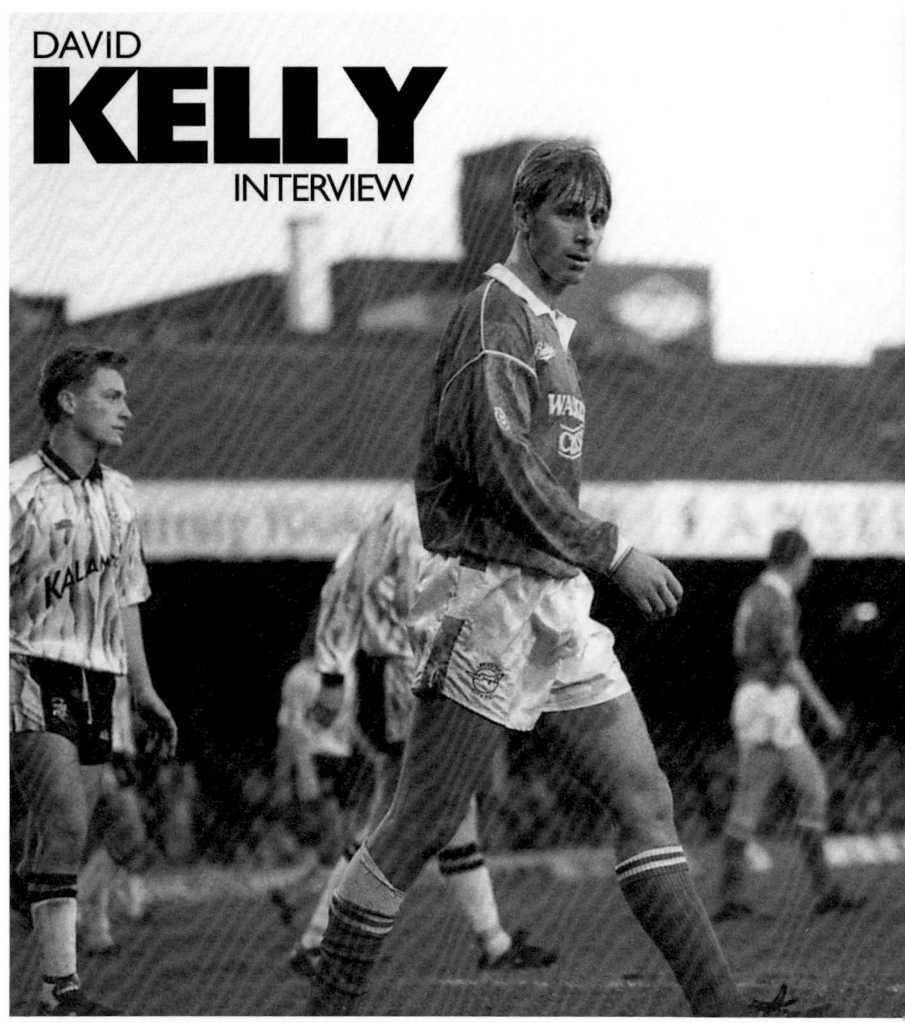

The FOX has a high noon meeting with former City striker David Kelly in a Wetherspoon's near Sutton Coldfield...

FOX: It is remarkable that you had a career as a footballer after suffering Legg-Calve-Perthes disease as a kid...
DK: Yes, I was definitely impaired until I was about 10. When I was about 5 I jumped out of a tree at my grandparents' caravan and my mum thought I'd broken my leg. But the doctors recognised that my bones weren't growing properly. It is a disease that attacks the hip, I was in plaster a lot. My left hip didn't grow, but my right hip was growing normally. So they had to split my legs and put a metal bar across to stabilise it. It was like that for ages. To get me to bed my old fella had to pick me up by the bar and drag me up the stairs. Every

DAVID KELLY

was aching I'd go in goal.
FOX: What team did you support as a kid?
DK: Albion! Cyrille Regis was my hero. I absolutely loved him. Moving on a few years I was playing for Wolves and Graham Turner said to me: "I'm signing someone who you are going to like tomorrow."
I said: "Okay, who is it?"
He said: "I can't tell you yet, you'll see tomorrow."
The next day Cyrille gets out of his car and I ran across the car park like a 10-year-old and gave him a hug.
In the dressing room Andy Thompson was sitting next to Cyrille and I said to him, "You need to move because I need to sit next to Cyrille." Poor Andy had been there years, but I made him move.
After a couple of weeks Cyrille took me to one side and said: "Look Ned, you are going to have to stop hugging and kissing me. It's getting embarrassing."
What could I do? I loved him.
Whenever I played with someone who'd been at the Albion I would always interrogate them about what the club had been like at the time. Ultimately I was a football supporter who had the fortune to be good enough to play.

FOX: In your early days you played for Alvechurch, how did you cope with that slope?

DK: If we were kicking from right to left as you come out of the tunnel then I'd go over to the right because you'd be playing downhill all through the half. You'd get used to it. Pitches were crap then; these days you'll have people working on them all day every day. Alvechurch, Redditch, even Leicester. After the first couple of months of the season, Filbert Street would be mostly brown with a bit of green round

now and again it would snap and back down the stairs I'd go. I was on crutches for a long time. It is still an awkward thing to get, but technology has made it much easier these days. I spent a lot of my junior school years with a metal bar going from my shoe to my back keeping my leg suspended. It wasn't easy to get around but it was what it was and I got on with it. I used to play football like that, and if my leg the edges. These days they have those lights that they put on them and they are all immaculate.

FOX: Was there a moment when you realised you were good enough to play professional football?

DK: No, absolutely not. When I was a teenager I played for the school in the week and three other teams at the weekend, Saturday morning, Sunday morning and Sunday afternoon. I played for Bartley Green Boys in the Sunday League and we were brilliant. Always top or second in the league. We'd beat teams 14 or 15-0 and I'd score eight. We were a really strong team with some great players. From about 12 to 14 I was picked up by the Albion and I trained with them and played a few games. And then one day it was 'thanks for coming, you're not quite good enough, off you pop.'

That's how it was. You'd turn up for training and think 'Where's that kid who was here last week?' Nobody knew and you'd never see them again. That's how brutal it was.

I went to Alvechurch, I just wanted to play football. I wasn't that bothered about training; I just wanted to play. I was obsessed with playing and scoring goals.

FOX: How did you end up at Walsall?

DK: There was a guy called Alan Miller who was a school teacher and ran the school district teams. He was given the youth team job at Alvechurch and he took a lot of the district players with him. It was a good team and scouts from Wolves and Walsall used to come and watch us. I got a three game trial period with Wolves which didn't come to anything. But then Walsall gave me a trial and I played in a Youth Cup game at Hillsborough. We beat Sheffield Wednesday 3-1 and I scored twice. Alan Buckley offered me a contract. At the same time Alvechurch moved me straight from the youth team to the first team and wanted me to sign a contract. I said to them, "No you're alright, I'll stay as I am." They knew Walsall were after me.

FOX: You did very well at Walsall, and then had a trial with Bayern Munich?

DK: Yes, Walsall got promoted and my contract was coming to an end. I thought I'd be moving on.

I've never had an agent, but this agent approached me and told me a few big clubs were interested, and also Bayern Munich wanted me to go for a trial.

> *I was in the car for an hour, going round in circles, on the wrong side of the road, sweating. I must have stopped and asked a dozen people.*

I flew over there with my girlfriend, now my wife, no agent. We were met at the airport by someone holding up a sign with my name on it. I couldn't speak a word of German and he couldn't speak English so he just sort of ushered us along. They put us in a hotel and said they'd come and pick

us up in the morning, or did we want a car? I didn't want to be stuck in the hotel all day so I said, "We'll have a car." They gave me a top of the range BMW, left hand drive, which I'd never driven before.
The training ground wasn't far away but I looked on a map and it looked a bit tricky. So I got up at 7 for training at 10. I am never late for anything, always early. I left at 8 for a 20-minute journey.
I was in the car for an hour, going round in circles, on the wrong side of the road, sweating. I must have stopped and asked a dozen people, but wasn't getting anywhere. I thought 'F**king hell! I've come all this way for a trial and I can't get there!'
I got there in the end. I played a couple of friendlies for them, scored a few goals. I thought I'd done well and the agent contacted me. He said, "They want to sign you, but they already have two foreigners, so they want to send you on loan to another German club for a season."
They planned to move Johnny Ekström on, the Swedish striker. When I went in the dressing room he said, "Ahh, you're here to replace me!" We hit it off and got on well, partly because he could speak English.

MERCURY SPORT SOCCER

Hot-shot Kelly

They offered me a contract but I didn't fancy going on loan. And if Johnny had a great season then they wouldn't want to get rid of him. So I binned them off. I did get a lovely kit bag though. The kit man dumped it next to me on the first day. A big bag full of Adidas stuff: tracksuit, t-shirt, kit, shorts, boots, training shoes, flip flops. I took that home with me.

FOX: You ended up signing for West Ham...

DK: Yes, the Hammers. Or the Unhappy Hammers as it turned out.

FOX: You got a lot of stick from the West Ham fans, is it possible for a player to block that out?

DK: No, I've heard players say that, but it is absolute bollocks in my opinion. I got absolutely hammered. It was partly because there was a big divide in the dressing room. There were some superb older players like Liam Brady, Alvin Martin, Phil Parkes, Alan Devonshire. But then you had Paul Ince, Stevie Potts, Julian Dicks, all these young lads with new contracts who were getting good money. But nothing in between. The older lads were coming to the end of their time and trying to get new contracts but West Ham weren't offering them anything. I signed along with Alan Knight, the goalkeeper, and as the new lads we seemed to get the blame for everything. Now, I was shit at West Ham, I don't deny that, it just didn't happen for me there. But I didn't think it was a good dressing room and I didn't enjoy it. That's my opinion. I said to Clair after a week or so, "This is going to be hard work," and it was.

I signed for West Ham because I really liked John Lyall when I met him, but he was gone within a few months and Lou Macari arrived. I didn't get on with him. He took us to Epping Forest for a run and after one lap all the older players were sitting down. Alan Devonshire said, "We don't run round the forest." Lou had done well at Stoke, but he didn't last long at West Ham. Then Billy Bonds came in and he was great. He said to me, "It's not working for you here, I'm going to let you go."

FOX: And then you arrived at Leicester. Did you have any options at the time?

DK: Yes, I did. But I liked David Pleat, he was obsessed with football, like me. Tommy Wright was the same. He was the most football-obsessed footballer I had ever met. He watched football all day, Italian, Spanish, anything he could watch. And he'd have arguments with Pleaty over tactics all the time. They would bicker with each other about football all day.

But it was a great dressing room, full of good people. Ali Mauchlen, Northy, Carl Muggleton, Millsy, Walshy was a brilliant lad. There was no divide. Ali ruled the dressing room, but it wasn't us and them. There was no one who wasn't speaking to someone else. And I thought straight away that I liked it there. Decent people. With a couple more signings I think it could have been a really good team.

FOX: David Pleat had a great reputation as a coach, why do you think it didn't work for him at Leicester?

DK: I just think he didn't have the squad depth. We had a good team, but we didn't have another good team. If an important player was out then they were missed because the back-up wasn't there. I mean we had Gary McAllister, who went to Leeds and won the league. If he was out there was nothing like him.

FOX: How did you feel when David Pleat got sacked?

DK: I was very disappointed for him, but we just weren't getting the results. Gordon Lee took over but we just kept going along the same really. He didn't change much. And then Brian Little came in and changed everything. New players, new training regimes, new rules. Put your flip flops on and don't walk around in your bare feet. Lots of silly little things that actually add up to making things better.

FOX: The biggest game in your time at Leicester saw us beat Oxford to avoid

was half decent as well.

I've been relegated a couple of times and it is extremely depressing. You have to accept that you are part of the reason for the club going down. And if you survive you are part of the reason you survived. After that game there was a sense of enormous relief. The build up to the last four or five games of the season was 'this club have never been in that league' so there was a lot of pressure on the players and the staff.

FOX: You scored 22 goals on 66 games for City, which mirrors your career record of a goal every three games. Are you happy with that?

DK: Yes, I think so. I'd like to have scored a goal every game like Ronaldo, of course, but I'm grateful for what I've got. I've had a career playing football with my mates. How good does it get? The thing I have always most wanted to do, and you end up getting paid for doing it. It's a dream job. And I love coaching too, getting paid for telling other people what to do is great.

FOX: Which strikers did you enjoy playing with?

DK: I liked playing with Steve Bull, although it didn't happen that often as he was injured when I arrived. I remember standing there waiting for a corner to come over and Bully said: "What are you doing?" I said, "I'm waiting for this corner to come over." He said, "F**king move! You're never going to score if you stand still." If you watched him he was always on the move. Him and Walshy were obsessed with each other. I think the world of both

> *It was a great dressing room, full of good people. Ali Mauchlen, Northy, Carl Muggleton, Millsy, Walshy was a brilliant lad.*

relegation to the third division. You and Tony James both went for the ball at the same time to score the only goal. Did you get anything on it?

DK: Yes, of course I did, I'm a striker! TJ

of them but they were always trying to kick lumps out of each other.

Richard O'Kelly and Trevor Christie at Walsall. They were both older players who knew the game and they took a lot of stick for me. They bore the brunt of challenges holding the ball up for me and taught me a lot.

I think me and Don Goodman complemented each other quite well.

We were both busy, not rapid, but quick enough and both decent in the air.

Trevor Peacock at Newcastle was a clever little player who helped me out. And Andy Cole was as obsessed with scoring as me.

FOX: Which defenders did you hate playing against?

DK: Walshy! Even in training. He wasn't trying to be horrible, he just was horrible. If he was marking you, he'd be looking at the ball and go past you and just bash into you. I'd say, "What are you doing?" He'd say, "What do you mean?" I genuinely don't think he knew he was doing it. He just thought, 'there's the ball I'm going to run there' and he didn't really notice anything that was in the way.

Brian Kilcline was another one. I think he was just clumsy, he'd tread on your heel and have no idea that he'd done it. Doug Rougvie in my early days at Walsall. I got sent off playing against him. I gave him a good shove and he never moved an inch. I thought 'f**k me, I'm in trouble now!' He ripped me in two so I booted him and got sent off. Mick McCarthy was another horrible one. But the best I have played against or trained with was Paul McGrath, by a million miles. What a player he was.

FOX: You didn't seem to get on with Brian Little when he came to Leicester and you were once fined a week's wages, what was that about?

DK: I liked Brian. He was enthusiastic and I remembered watching him play for Villa, and he was bloody good. He was quite clear in how he wanted us to play and his instructions were very clear.

Now, one game I was playing in I'd scored two goals and with about 20 minutes to go my number comes up. I wasn't happy because I was on a hat trick and I thought, 'I'm not going off.'

The ref comes over and says "Come on Ned, you've got to go." As I went over to the bench I held up two fingers to say 'I've scored twice' but it didn't look good; it looked like I was giving him the vees. I went down the tunnel with steam coming

> *Straight in the dressing room, grabbed all my stuff and went out into the car park and drove home in my kit. All the way to Essex. I'd completely lost it.*

out of my ears, straight in the dressing room, grabbed all my stuff and went out into the car park and drove home in my kit. All the way to Essex. I'd completely lost it.

When I got in the house, Clair said: "What

have you done?"
I said: "What do you mean?"
She said, "Well, for one, you are in your kit. And two, the club have phoned and want you in at 9 tomorrow morning."
So there I was the following morning driving into the old Filbert Street car park the following morning and Brian turns up at exactly the same time. We drive up to each other and get out of the cars. I said: "Gaffer! Why would you sub me?" He said, "The game was finished, you'd played really well, I was just trying to kill the game off. You've got to realise it isn't just about you, it's about the rest of the team." I said, "But you don't get many opportunities for a hat trick."
He said: "Okay, I get that, and maybe it will be something I think about in the future. But you're fined a week's wages."
We were in the car park for no longer than three minutes, I'd driven from Essex, he'd driven from Stoke.

FOX: How would the older, wiser coach David Kelly deal with that?
DK: Same way Brian did!
I've always been a coach, never a manager so I have always been that sort of buffer between the players and the manager.

FOX: It wasn't long before you left Leicester, how did that come about?
DK: Well Flash came in, Colin Gordon. I hadn't scored for seven or eight games and Brian told me I'd be starting on the bench. I told him you were only ten seconds away from your next goal, but I was out and Flash was in. On Monday I went into Brian's office and told him if he wasn't going to play me then I wanted to leave. He said, "Ned! I've only left you out for one game!"
The following game I was out again and Flash scored two. So I was in again on Monday. I told him I wasn't hanging around for weeks if I wasn't in the first

team. Flash and Paul Kitson were doing quite well. He said, "Okay, if that's the route you want to go."
Then suddenly Wolves, Newcastle and Sunderland were all interested, he must have put the word out.
They were all struggling near the bottom of the Second Division at the time and I went and spoke to all of them. I liked Ossie Ardiles at Newcastle. I phoned my uncle up to see what he thought and he said: "If you wear that number 9 shirt at Newcastle and score a load of goals up there, you'll be remembered forever. There's a difference."
So I phoned Ossie up and told him I was coming. I did actually end up going to both Wolves and Sunderland in the end. This was at the time that Sir John Hall was taking over at Newcastle and there were soon rumours that Ossie would be going. But there were no rumours about Kevin Keegan coming in. I think that deal happened in two or three days. And when he arrived it was like someone had

lit the blue touch paper and the whole city erupted. It was like the Messiah coming back.
But we were in trouble towards the end of the season. We survived on the last day of the season at Filbert Street, but the game that really did it was Portsmouth the week before.

FOX: You scored the winner against Portsmouth and the fans had a tifo display last week in your honour...
DK: I was at the game and had no idea it was going to happen. It was incredible. My uncle was right!
I watch a lot of football and I'm welcomed back to all my old clubs. People are really nice.

FOX: How did you come to leave Newcastle?
DK: We'd won the league with three games to go. After the last game I'd collected all my stuff and went home to Birmingham and then we were going straight on holiday. On the way down Kevin Keegan phoned me on my great big car phone and said "Where are you?" I'd got as far as Ferry Bridge. He said: "I need to have a chat with you." I said, "Are you selling me?" He said: "Just pull over." I went to a hotel and rang him back from there. He said: "I've had a bit of interest in you. I'm signing someone tomorrow and it will mean your playing time will be more limited."
I said: "Who are you signing?"
He said: "I can't tell you that, it isn't done yet."
I said: "Well if you don't tell me I'm not leaving."
Kevin said: "I can't f**king do that! It's top secret."
I said: "I won't tell anybody."
I could hear him mumbling to Terry McDermott in the background.
This went on for a while and then he said: "Look, I know if you aren't playing you aren't going to be happy and you'll be a nightmare for me. I'm signing Peter

Beardsley."
I said: "F**king hell Gaffer! I'd play Peter Beardsley instead of David Kelly."
I went and signed for Wolves, which I was delighted to do.
All my Albion mates thought I was Judas, but I had no qualms about it.

FOX: You played 26 games for Ireland. Did you have to choose between England and Ireland?

DK: When I was at Walsall I got a letter from the FA calling me up for an U21s game against Czechoslovakia. Before that, we had a game at Rotherham, we won and I scored. After the game Walsall manager Tommy Coakley said: "There's somebody who wants to have a chat with you. Jack Charlton is upstairs."
I went up to the boardroom which was a cloud of cigar smoke and I was peering through it trying to see him. Then this hand came up and waved. I went over and there was Jack and Maurice Setters his assistant with pints and cigars. I was standing behind them and Jack turned round and said: "Do you want to come and play for us son?" I said: "Under-21s or first team?" He said: "First team. We're playing Israel a week on Wednesday. You've scored enough goals now, we want you in our squad."
I said: "Okay, I'm in." He said: "Right, I'll send you a letter." Then the two of them turned round and I was left standing behind them. I thought, right I can go now. The lads were all waiting for me on the team bus and gave me a round of applause.
I phoned my dad, who was a functioning alcoholic, to tell him I'd been picked for Ireland and he said: "F**king brilliant! We're going to Dublin!"
I got a hat trick on my debut against Israel at Dalymount Park and was blessed to spent the next ten years going round the world playing football with my mates. I only played 26 games in that time, but that didn't matter to me, I was travelling all round the world with a great bunch of lads. Jack created a great dressing room and protected everybody.
Jack and Maurice used to go by the names. If there was a Kelly or an O'Reilly or any Irish name they would see if they were qualified. I don't know how they found Tony Cascarino.

FOX: You scored against England in the game that was abandoned due to crowd trouble. Did you get to keep that goal?

DK: In my head, yes. But in the records I'm told not. One of the pricks that was involved in that was a Wolves fan, and I happened to be going into reception at the same time as he was coming in to have his season ticket taken off him and get his banning order. I said "You're one of those w***kers that ruined the game," and he just stared at the floor. It was an awful night, I remember as we were coming off the pitch there was this metal bar sticking out of the pitch from a broken seat. They could have killed someone.

FOX: Tell us about meeting the Pope.

DK: The Pope was brilliant! The Bishop of Belfast always came along with the national team and some of the lads used to have Mass. Now, I'm not a Mass person. Right at the start of Italia 90 someone had said if we get to Rome then we need to go and see the Pope.
So we get through the group, and then we get past Romania on penalties and then

we are playing Italy in Rome and it is all getting real. It is all arranged and we go to the Vatican, we don't go in the front where everyone queues up, we are taken in the back way past all these private rooms. We are led into this big room and as it happens I find myself on the front row, typical of me, with Chris Hughton, Charlie the kit man and Jack. Some of the more religious members of the squad behind us, are going, "Hey Kels! Come on. Swap with one of us. Be fair." I turned round to them and said: "F**k right off!"

The Pope was really lovely and it was a great moment. My mum lives in a warden controlled place now and she has a picture of me and the Pope next to her door. My punishment from the rest of the squad for not moving was to take the official photographers album round the hotel so everyone could order their photos. It took me hours. When I took the orders back to him the photographer gave me the album and said, "Here, I don't need this anymore." So even doing my penance meant that I got all the photos for free. They all paid for theirs!

FOX: Your path with Leicester crossed again in the 2000 League Cup Final...

DK: Yes, I loved it at Tranmere. I scored the equaliser. A free-kick came in and big Gary Jones nodded it down and I smashed it in. I knew Matt Elliott quite well through a mutual friend who was at that game. So one of his mates scored one and the other scored two. We had a great cup run to the final.

I was in the park with the dogs when I got a phone call from John Aldridge. He said: "Do you want to come and play for us?" Kevin Sheedy was his assistant and Les Parry was the physio, so I knew all of them. I said: "I ain't moving," because I'd just moved back to Sutton, "I'll drive up." He'd signed Paul Cook and Andy Thompson so I shared cars with them. It ended up being the only club where I served my full three year contract. Everywhere else I had left.

FOX: Who were the stand out managers and coaches from your career?

DK: Well, not Lou Macari because I couldn't stand him. Or Eric Black, who was hopeless.
I loved Jack Charlton, because he was brilliant. He was all about the group. Graham Taylor, I didn't realise how good he was until I left Wolves.
I liked David Pleat.

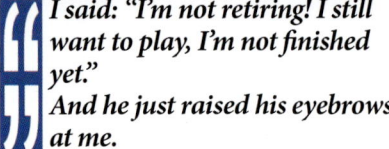
I said: "I'm not retiring! I still want to play, I'm not finished yet."
And he just raised his eyebrows at me.

Aldo was good but it was sometimes difficult because he was my mate. And you can't tell him to f**k off when he's your gaffer.
And Billy Davies at Motherwell. He's a brilliant manager.
And I had 18 months as assistant to Neil Warnock at Sheffield United. He was great.

He'd have a day off and trust me to take over training.

FOX: How did you know when it was time to retire?
DK: I didn't!
I was playing at Sheffield United and around Christmas Neil said to me "I'm signing Carl Asaba. I want you to teach him how to play for a bit and then I want you as a coach next season."
I said: "I'm not retiring! I still want to play, I'm not finished yet."
And he just raised his eyebrows at me.
I went to Motherwell under Billy Davies, but he got the sack after a few months. Eric Black came in and I had a massive row with him. Then I went to Mansfield and I played about eight games and we got promoted.
I felt like I was finished after that, but the owner of Derry City, Jim Roddy, rang me and said, "Fly over here, I'll pick you up, play the game, then we'll have a night out and I'll drop you at the airport the next day."
It sounded okay and the money was good, but he didn't tell me it was an hour and a half in the car at the time! By the end of that season I knew I was finished.
While I was playing for Derry I met the Tranmere manager Ray Mathias at a Leicester game. He offered me a coaching job and said, "I need someone who's going to tell me what they think, I've got too many people who aren't disagreeing with me." I said, "Don't worry Ray, I can do that!"

FOX: What do you miss about playing?
DK: The group of players. Scoring goals. I joined in for years and years as a coach so I could keep scoring goals, but my knees are shot now. I'm too old and I don't want to hurt myself, but I miss playing all the time. All the time.

FOX: What were your career highlights?
DK: Scoring for Newcastle against Portsmouth to avoid relegation.
My first international goal for Ireland.
The League Cup Final goal against Leicester.
And sorry, a great diving header for Wolves also against Leicester in the FA Cup.
If I thought about it for long enough I'd probably come up with about 30 others.

FOX: Are you currently in the game?
DK: No, I'm looking. But after Covid and with the world currently being in the shit it's hard. Everyone is cutting down and I get that. But if I don't get back in, that's fine because the game doesn't owe me anything. How lucky have I been? I've been involved in football since 1983 and now it is 2022. I've had a great time in the game. □

UNFORGETTABLES

"Well played, Kanté." These three words became my mantra in the title-winning season, or a stuck record as my children would claim. I'd say it multiple times each game as he manoeuvred imperiously just in front of the back four. My son soon turned to me and said, "Dad, you like Kanté, don't you?"

Love or complete adoration were probably better words. I simply thought he was the greatest player I had ever seen in a City shirt. How he would be everywhere in midfield. He'd make a tackle, gain possession and lay it off simply, but effectively. He'd never commit a foul. If Vardy and Mahrez were our Eric Morecambes, Kanté was our Ernie Wise. Equally diminutive, never in the main glare but we all knew the whole thing would never work without him.

When City scored and the players embraced like Roman gladiators celebrating victoriously, the steam rising from their massed bodies, Kanté would always be the last to join in. With a beaming smile, full of teeth and pointy cheekbones, he would cling to a couple of torsos in the huddle and, being the shortest in the team, press a single cheek against somebody's shoulder or back. Similar to when a young child joins in a celebration started by elder siblings, unaware what the celebration is about but wanting to share the joy anyway. He would be the last there but the first to leave and trot back to his position, head down, totally focused on the re-start.

It's well-known that Kanté came from lower league obscurity. Three years before winning the Premier League, he was playing in the ninth tier of the French leagues, spent one year playing in Ligue 1 at Caen before head of recruitment, Steve Walsh, convinced new manager Claudio Ranieri to take a punt on the 24-year-old midfielder. Walsh had been monitoring Kanté for a couple of years, but Ranieri continued to raise questions over his weight and height. Ranieri started the season with Danny Drinkwater in central midfield and another new signing, Gokan Inler, coming from the more physical Serie A.

Walsh wasn't put off and the story goes that he would walk behind the manager at training and whisper the words "Kanté, Kanté" over again. If Kanté's vital measurements didn't convince Ranieri, his performance stats did. After his single year in Ligue 1 Kanté had won the ball back more times than anyone in any other top European league and was described by *L'Equipe* as "a monster" after inspiring Caen to come from 2-0 down to Marseille with 25 minutes remaining to win 3-2. "He strolled between Marseille's lines like a fish through water," wrote the French sports daily. Quite possibly the first sportsman ever to be likened to a monster and a fish in the same paragraph.

I've only had to do a double-take on a footballer twice. The first was when Gary Taylor-Fletcher made his City debut. I thought the well-built, former roofer was a over-sized mascot or was the lucky winner of a raffle prize to warm up with the players. The second was when Kanté made his debut at the King Power. He looked like a ballboy gently returning the ball to the players and was even mistaken for an Academy player by security staff.

A failure to keep a clean sheet in the first nine games convinced Ranieri to give Kanté his first start alongside Drinkwater. The result was a 1-0 home win against Crystal Palace and, as promised, the manager took the team out for a pizza. The Italian, the Frenchman and Leicester never looked back.

Kanté fitted the Leicester profile of journeymen and rejects too, having being rejected by the French FA's academy at Clairefontaine and over-looked by Arsene Wenger despite being recommended by one of the Arsenal manager's best friends. He was certainly understated off the pitch too. I hardly ever heard him talk publicly, I've no idea if he was married at the time, he drove a Mini and he attended local mosques visiting fellow worshippers' homes to eat biryani and play FIFA.

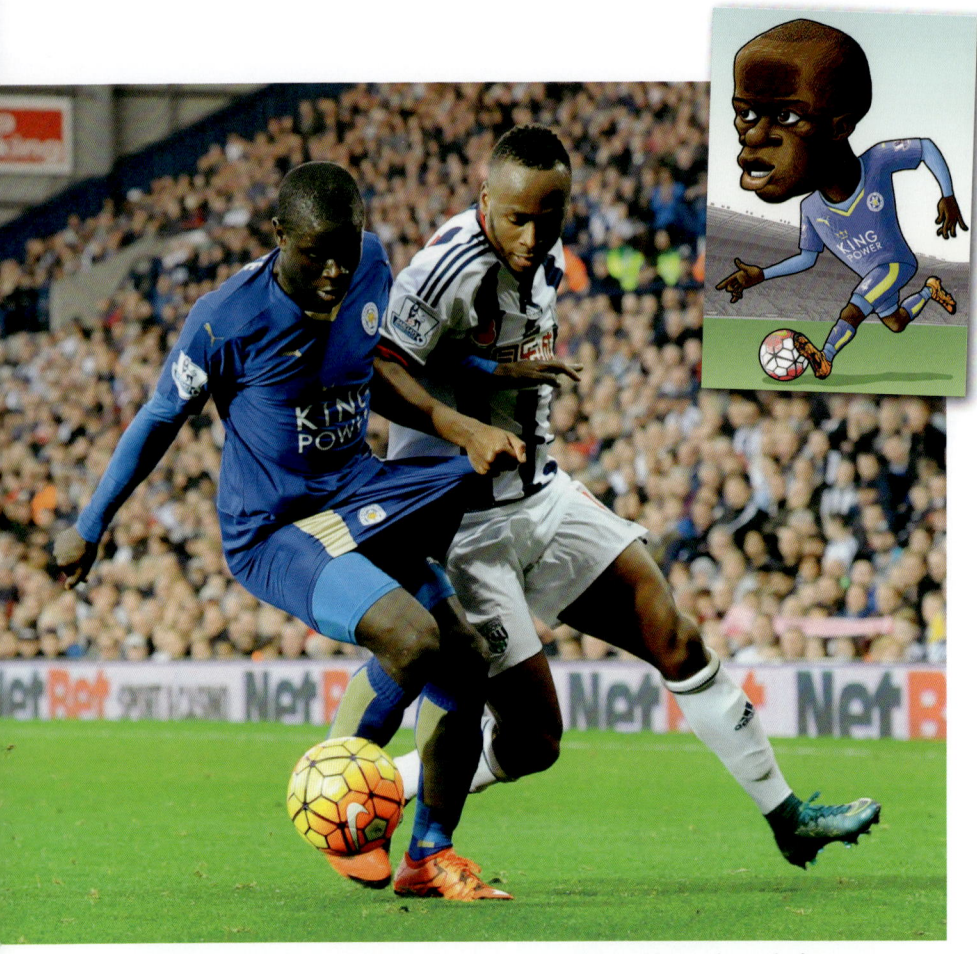

Modern football is defined by data and Kanté had the best defensive stats in 2015/16. By the end of his only season with City he had managed 31 more tackles and 15 more interceptions than any other player. Another stat made in onto t-shirts being sold outside the ground: "70% of the earth is covered by water," I'll let you finish the rest. Ranieri even joked with him: "One day, I'm going to see you cross the ball, and then finish the cross with a header yourself!"

My favourite stat: On 3 August 2015 Kanté signed for Leicester, 273 days later the Premier League was won.

We loved him. The end of season Football Writers and PFA awards might have gone to Vardy and Mahrez but subscribers to The FOX Fanzine chose Kanté as their Player of the Season. We knew. Unfortunately, Chelsea knew too and he was soon off to win Champions Leagues and a World Cup.

I'll leave the final words to Steve Walsh discussing team formations: "We play with Drinkwater in the middle and Kanté either side."

Well played and Unforgettable.

Rob Coe

STEVE SMITH

The Foxes Trust Board members past and present and former posters on the FOX Fanzine message board were all very sad to hear the news over the summer of Steve's passing after a second stroke at the age of 54.

I first got to know Steve via his amusing and debate provoking posts as both Masked Avenger and Dancing Fox on the message board; however I met him for the first time in the Half Time Orange as a team of fans started planning the formation of the Trust.

As we both joined the working party interim board I quickly appreciated his great sense of humour while at the same time delivering what needed to be done. He was particularly effective engaging with fellow fans outside the ground prior to games, whether fund raising or signing up members. Steve formed part of the fundraising team initially, but was also passionate about preserving the heritage of the club, meeting Christine Smeaton who had kept many artefacts at home, with the aim of them being made available to fans in the future. He promised we would make this happen, while also having regular dialogue with the initial developers of our old Filbert Street home and the local council to ensure this was recognised, with the naming of Lineker Road.

My favourite memory of Steve summed him up perfectly. This was in the early days of the Trust when getting media coverage to encourage fans to become Trust members or donate was key. At that time, we had great success with coverage locally other than on 'local' commercial radio, where there was an evening football phone-in with Darren Fletcher and Garry Birtles that had good listener numbers, but was Forest obsessed and gave City little air time despite being in administration. Both Steve and I tried to get on without success much to our frustration. So, one day Steve rang me up, and said "I've got a plan" and then rang off, I could tell he had a big grin on his face.

As I drove home that evening listening to the show, an ardent Forest fan called Barry rang in, and proceeded to say how funny Leicester's situation was and he hoped we'd go out of existence. The presenters then asked for Leicester fans' reaction, so I quickly rang up and got on air for the first time and explained that no fan wants to see the loss of their club and got over the messages we had wanted to do for weeks.

Soon afterwards another 'Forest' fan called, saying that I had talked a lot of sense and that fellow Forest fans should be backing Leicester fans, and the rest of the callers on that show seemed to agree.

So, having mentioned the character creation on the message boards earlier, I don't think I need to explain to you who the two Forest fans really were. Steve used both characters again in subsequent shows to keep the topic being discussed.

The Trust Board missed Steve's input following his first stroke in late 2005 but he remained interested and despite his limited communication skills frequently asked about the Trust. It was great to play Walking Football with Steve in recent years where he became very popular with those taking part.

It was an honour to know Steve and I'm sure, like so many who knew him would say, he had a positive contribution to my life.

Ian Bason

ONE FOX ON A SHIRT... a badge history

These days, a badge is an essential part of a football club's identity, whether it be competing in Champions League or Sunday League.

We are used to seeing the Holy Trinity of club crest, kit manufacturer's logo and shirt sponsor's advert on the players' chests as has been the case for some four decades now. But of course this this wasn't always the way. In a time before the commercialism of the sport even a club badge wasn't considered necessary as illustrated by Leicester City.

Among the earliest photos of Leicester Fosse there is a team group of Victorian players from the 1890/91 season, where four members of the team are sporting the city coat of arms on their jerseys. This was a wyvern perched above the cinquefoil. A wyvern is a two-legged dragon which stems from the Earls of Leicester heraldry stretching back to the 13th century. If you go for a walk round Leicester and keep your gaze upwards

you will see several wyverns, especially on New Walk, around Victoria Park and in Town Hall Square.

A season ticket from the 1894/95 season bears the same coat of arms, which suggests that this was officially the club's first badge, but they soon fell out of favour on the shirts. The 1892/93 team group shows just one player, Ernest 'Snooks' Nuttall, wearing the badge and after that they disappear altogether.

For half a century the club did without a club crest altogether. From the evidence we have seen the club letterheads through the first half of the 20th Century had some wonderfully jaunty art deco style typeface, but no logo. But then, in July 1948, the City board decided that a new badge should be commissioned and worn on the players' shirts for the 1948/49 season, the third since the end of World War II.

It was decided that the new crest should reflect the fox-hunting traditions of Leicestershire and the artist produced a rather beautiful rendition of a fox's head over crossed riding crops, based on the head of an actual fox killed by the Atherstone Hunt. Rather less beautiful was the simplified version that was used on the shirts, you can only imagine the artist's feelings on seeing it, but perhaps the fact that it had to be embroidered had to be borne in mind.

The new badge proved to be a lucky one as City progressed to Wembley for the first time ever, facing Wolves in the 1949 FA Cup Final. A 3-1 defeat saw the first of four losing finals, but we got there in the end.

Despite this success, the new badge didn't last long. The 1950/51 programme was adorned with a redesigned crest, a little closer to the original artist's work with the crossed crops, now surrounded by a shield with the legend 'L.C.F.C. LEICESTER CITY FOOTBALL CLUB.'

The team group photos from 1950/51 and 1951/52 show the squad in a mixture of the old and new badges, but by 1952 they are all uniformly wearing the new version on a white square. This badge would undergo various tweaks on the shirt over the decades but remained essentially the same club logo until 1983.

The rest of the 1950s saw City consistently turning out in the badge on a white square, until the start of the 1961/62 season when it was revamped into a shield shape which better suited the more streamlined collar of the '60s.

The shield shape and white background remained throughout the '60s, until the 1969 FA Cup Final when a special set of shirts was worn. The badge was woven directly onto the shirt meaning that it had a blue background with 'Wembley '69' embroidered beneath. City returned to the white badge for the start of the 1969/70 season, though later turned out in a style similar to the Cup Final shirt.

The Second Division Championship season of 1970/71 saw this style retained, as did the following season in the First Division, before a radical change came in 1972/73. Jimmy Bloomfield changed the home colours to all-white and the badge now appeared in a circle rather than a shield, though the badge in the programme and on club stationery stuck with tradition. The change of colour proved to be unpopular and after one season the home shirt reverted to blue, with a white button-up collar, though the circular badge remained.

After three seasons in this shirt a seismic shift arrived for 1976/77 with commercialism entering the arena. City's new Admiral strip had its logos sprinkled everywhere, but they retained the circular badge, moving it to a central position.

The Admiral kit lasted for three seasons before City switched to Umbro for the 1979/80 Second Division title-winning campaign under Jock Wallace, the fans were delighted to see the return of the

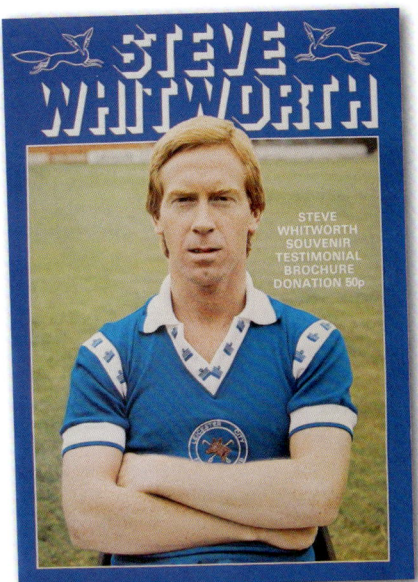

new modern logo and dropping the shield completely after a third of a century.

The new badge certainly wasn't an instant hit with the fans; it featured a graphic of what became known as the 'three-legged fox' and was accused of being 'weak-looking'. And as money began

shield badge. The Umbro version had a yellow fox and crossed crops, rather than the foxy brown of previous years. But this

proved to be the last outing for the shield badge.

In the summer of 1983 City went for a complete rebranding, introducing a

to speak louder in the game this was also the first shirt to have a shirt sponsor. The badge no longer had pride of place on the chest.

Shirt designs were now changed every couple of years and the three-legged fox was worn on three different Admiral shirts, a Scoreline and a Bukta before its brief reign ended in 1992. The latter added the wording 'Leicester City FC' round the badge.

1992 was a time of change at Filbert Street with Brian

The badge appeared on the first Fox Leisure shirt in the 1992/93 season in glorious isolation, but there were, inevitably, some tweaks to it in the following years. The '90s were a time of ostentatious shirt designs and a shield was added round the crest for the 94-96 and 96-98 Fox Leisure shirts. And on both the last Fox Leisure kit and the first Le Coq Sportif shirts at the turn of the century a wrong-looking wide margin was added.

Little and Barrie Pierpoint propelling the club forward on and off the field. Chris Lymn, designer, City fan and long time FOX contributor, was given the task of coming up with stronger club logo, and he delivered just that. The fox's head was back, in a more positive head-on position, though the controversial associations

When City left Filbert Street and moved to the Walkers Stadium in 2002, the badge was given a slight makeover, with a bolder typeface and thicker border. Though a more significant change was avoided when the supporters voted overwhelmingly against a proposal to revert back to the

with fox hunting were no longer present. Instead, the backdrop was now the city cinque foil, not seen since the early days of the Fosse, and more representative of the city, rather than just the county.

For a new badge, it went down well and has survived, with only the odd tweak, for thirty years now.

Leicester Fosse name.

The club badge remained unaltered until 2009, although when Jako produced the kit in 2007-09 it was housed within a white shield, reminiscent of the shield badge.

There was a drastic change in 2009-10 as the club celebrated its 125th Anniversary, but it was a temporary one. The fox was picked out in gold thread, with white cheeks, the words 'football club' were replaced by '1884-2009' and a banner was added to the bottom reading '125 years'.

The badge reverted back the following season, although the white remained on

the fox's muzzle, and there have been no changes in the King Power era until recently. During that time this badge has seen the club win a League Championship title, pull off the Great Escape, lift the Premier League trophy, compete in the Champions League, finally win the FA Cup and beat Champions Manchester City in the Community Shield.

Recent seasons have seen a trend towards Adidas using a monochrome

badge for away strips, most notably for the FA Cup Final in 2021. But for the 2022/23 season this was applied to the home shirt, with the club crest entirely in gold. And

sitting below the collar on the back of the shirt is old three-legs, proving that yesterday's unpopular badge can be today's nostalgia...

LETTERS

When we announced the end of the The FOX as a regular fanzine we were overwhelmed with an avalanche of letters and emails. Quite brought a tear to the eye. Here are as many as we could fit in. Thanks for your thanks.

'Thanks for 30+ years of The FOX - they've always been enjoyable, even through the dark days of Peter Taylor and Ian Holloway. Glad you're still doing an annual!' **Nick Jelley**

'I can't believe after nearly 35 years of coming through my letterboxes you will be no more, so sad. You are an institution, it's quite depressing but thanks so much for doing what you did for so long, end of an era.' **Nigel Wilby**

'Devastated to read The FOX will be no more. Proper football mag from proper football people. So sad. I know you have a bunch of other projects so all the best with those. Honestly mate, anyone who wants to understand what football is all about should turn off Sky Sports and read The FOX from the beginning, cover to cover. It's got everything.' **Wayne Barker**

'Many thanks Gary, assistant editors and contributors for 35 years of The FOX (225 issues, Summer Specials etc).
I fully understand the reasons for ending the regular printed issues but, as someone who's not online for several hours every day, I'll miss The FOX. But how fantastic that you've been able to chronicle the last six glorious and fantastic seasons of our great club. I'll also miss your facts - I hadn't realised that City have now achieved a top flight top half finish for the fifth season running - the best in our long history. Roll on The Fox Annual 2022!' **High Peak Fox**

'I can't say that I'm surprised that The FOX has run its course as a monthly/bi monthly magazine but I am disappointed and will miss it greatly! I have always looked forward to reading it from cover to cover, a great read... ah well!
UP THE CITY!!' **Ann Holyoak**

'I heard the news you're finishing The FOX. A sad day, but I'd rather look back and say what an amazing job you've done! I can tell my grandchildren I have every copy (from no.18 anyway) and/or sit and wait 'til the value goes through the roof and I can sell to fund a lavish lifestyle... Cheers for all you've done.
Up The City!' **Peter Dring**

'I was very sorry to read that the latest edition of The FOX is to be the last one and couldn't let this moment pass without passing on my thanks for 35 years of great reading.
The first two matches I can clearly

remember going to were City 5 Plymouth Argyle 0 (FA Cup 4th Round, 30/01/65) and City 0 Manchester United 5 (Division 1, 13/11/65), which, looking back, were an early sign of the ups and downs a life of supporting City would bring. So although, I think, I'm a little older than you, the majority of your City supporting life and the history and memories you write about mostly coincide with mine.

Whilst nothing will ever compare to the phenomenon of the 2015-16 season and The Greatest Day, 7 May 2016, nostalgia dictates that the Bloomfield years, closely followed by the O'Neill years gave me some of my best memories as a Leicester fan. My favourite ever players are Frankie Wortho (will always be No. 1), Jamie Vardy (the GOAT), Muzzy Izzet, Gary Lineker and Keith Weller. But we all know that the many years of 'thin' between the more occasional 'thick' made the success all the more meaningful and enjoyable.

I have always thought your fanzine approach to writing about our beloved club was spot on, that you 'got it'. Like family, we are fiercely loyal to our team but that doesn't mean we're not allowed to be critical (very, at times). We don't like it if others criticise, though! Underneath it all is that fantastic sense of humour that has been essential for supporting Leicester over the years. It was always good that my team, through The FOX, had a fantastic example of the fanzine movement, which has always been such a welcome antidote to the worst of the corporate excesses of modern professional football.

Like myself, my sons, Matt and Dan, are lifelong City supporters and in their cases, lifelong FOX readers too. We have all been subscribers for a good few years, now and we'll all miss the arrival of the latest edition and the following text exchanges or discussion on the latest content when we meet up at matches. With them now living in Sheffield and Tonbridge, and myself

having recently returned after eight years' exile in North Yorkshire, The FOX has also played a part in keeping us closer to home.

Thanks once again for all your efforts over the years on The FOX and please pass on my thanks to the rest of the team, in particular Simon Kimber who I always used to buy my copy from on the way to the ground, and have a quick chat with.

'The Big Blue Leicester City Scrapbook' 'Got, Not Got', 'Got, Not Got Leicester City' and 'Can't Buy that Feeling' are all on my bookshelves and you can be sure I'll be subscribing to 'The Fox Annual' too. With thanks and very best wishes.'

Ric Payne

'Thanks for the last 35 years and definitely understand your reasons to cease publication, sad though the loss will be of a quality magazine that has always been a critical friend of the club we love.
Will subscribe and look forward to the annual, good luck with it.
First thing I got published was my best ever City line up!
Which would now be in 4-4-2:
Banks, Fuchs, Walsh, Morgan, Whitworth, Weller, Cambiasso, Kante, Glover,

Worthington, Vardy. All the best Gary and thanks again, doubtless see you down Filbo in the future.' **Andy Betts**

'Well Gary, we've never met but you feel like an old friend as I have been a subscriber one way or another for around 30 years.
I fully understand your reasons for ending the regular fanzine and it feels like a good time to sign off – we've just about seen every high and low you could imagine but probably like you, I still find myself randomly smiling in the most unexpected places, when the memories of *that* season (and now the FA Cup too) pop up.
I just wanted to say that you have done far more than produce a fanzine – which lifts my heart a little, every time it appears amongst my post; you have created a platform for people to share their stories; their emotions and feel connected to the community of Leicester supporters - in a way in which no other magazine, media company or club institution would ever be able to do. I was so chuffed to have my piece about Orient away promotion day – I was sad to read about a fellow London supporter's club member (Colin Martin) passing away on Cup Final day but I only knew because of The FOX. I've loved the former player interviews and most of all I love the style, humility and humour of your content. I will most certainly be subscribing to the annual edition.
Thank you again.' **Paul Marcus**

'Gary, I've just stuck a cheque in the post for the Annual. As the renewal is the only time I use it, it's possibly the last time I'll use the cheque book as well as the last FOX!
I regret that you're ceasing publication - but I understand why. You have ended on a high, once again a great read.
I think I've pretty much been subscribing since the beginning, which is a journey taking me from Leicester to Gloucester and back to Staffordshire, kids, grandkids, and watching us being bloody awful at Twerton Park and going nowhere under Mr Pleat, to being still fairly awful at Rennes (apart from 10 minutes) but still going somewhere under Mr Rodgers.
You and your team should be very proud of what you have done over the years. Even our Wolves-supporting village postman started to recognise what the brown envelope contained - if only from the grin upon my face when it arrived. Much appreciated. Thank you.
Enjoy being just a fan from here onwards.' **Nick Bonser**

'I just wanted to make contact to say thanks to you and your team for all the enjoyment your fanzine has brought me over the years. I really appreciate it. I'm looking forward to the Annual.
Best of Luck & Up the City!' **Stu Teasdale**

'I've just opened up the May 225 issue, and I've just read the Editorial and the news about the fanzine coming to an end. I just wanted to say, that you and the team have done a brilliant job over the years, and it only seems like yesterday that I was religiously purchasing the fanzine from you on the old Filbo carpark, before hitting Pen 3 or 4, depending on the mood and company - great days! Even though the football was tough to watch at times. I'm not sure if I have every single copy, but I can't be far off! Quite a few will be stuck in boxes somewhere, due to the many moves that I've undertaken over the years, thanks to my profession. I might even get round to sorting them all out one day. Anyway, I'm really glad it's not 'final' as such, and I'm looking forward to the Annual. Look after yourself and, as always, Up the City!' **Stewart Gee**

'Issue Number 225 dropped through my letterbox this morning, and I read that it was to be the final issue.
I would just like to say a big thank you to you for the countless hours of work, and painstaking effort that you have put in over the past 35 years. The FOX has always been an excellent read, and many articles down the years have brought a smile to my face. We have seen many ups and downs along the way following our beloved City, but the past few years have certainly been the halcyon days. It seems a long time ago since going to Yeovil on a Monday night, not to mention Hartlepool on a Tuesday night!
Gary, I would like to wish you all the very best for the future, and again sincere thanks for your massive and outstanding contribution towards the enjoyment of all true City supporters. I shall be dropping a cheque in the post to you for The Fox Annual 2022.' **Peter Johnson**

'As a Foxile I am especially sad at seeing the last FOX fanzine. I was a regular throughout nearly all the 42 years I lived and worked in Leicester and it remained a great contact with the club.

At least we have Robbie Savage here in Macclesfield doing great work and Macclesfield were Champions of their League this year. My other pals round here are ecstatic at Stockport County's return to the EFL – a reminder of a boring 0-0 draw with LCFC at Edgeley Park in the third tier days. The most interesting thing in that match was watching the planes coming in to land at Manchester Airport. Thanks so much for all your hard work over 35 years. It really is appreciated.
Robert Bracegirdle

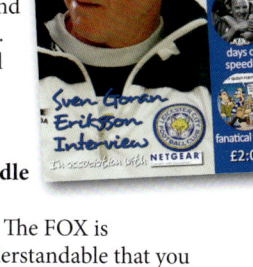

'Although it is sad that The FOX is finishing it is fully understandable that you feel it is time for it to end. At least we have the Premier League and FA Cup tucked under our arms and who would ever have thought that?
My favourite sections of The FOX have been the interviews with former players and officials and also the Fanatical Frank strip. In recent years I've not enjoyed the letters page so much. As with social media these days people just seem to rant and rave and use bad language. Maybe I'm a bit old fashioned.
Well done to you and your team for keeping us entertained over the years. I look forward to the Annual.
Best wishes.' **Ed Thomas**

'As usual I looked forward to reading The FOX and naturally I was disappointed to read that you're calling time. But I

can fully understand why. Times move on I guess. You should be proud of your achievement in producing The FOX all these years. You always seemed to have your finger on the pulse and the various features have been brilliant. I loved the humour as well. That's what it was all about, not taking ourselves too seriously. I loved it, especially as I have been an exile since 1981.
I've been watching the City since 1965, some dark days and some bloody marvellous ones too – unbelievable ones. All this covered so well by yourself.
I was lucky enough to discover The FOX back in 1987. I have issue No 2 and virtually all of them since. I went to a Programme Fair in the old Main Stand and bought a copy. I was hooked! Looking back at the early ones I loved the Jimmy Quinn Puzzle Page (No 5), The Subbuteo Years (No 7) and The Ugliest Goalie in the Midlands (No 8) – absolute genius.
Anyway, just wanted to say thanks – great stuff, great laughs.'   **Adrian Hyde**

'So sorry to hear The FOX's time has come to an end. I have been away from Leicestershire since I was 22 (I'm 53 now!) and from Brum to Cheltenham, to London to St Albans and through the thick or the very thin of being a Foxes fan your fanzine has been an important part of my life. Good luck, thank you and looking forward to the Annual.'   **Sophie Brookes**

'I would like to thank you, Simon & co for all the work you have put into the fanzine for so many years. I think I started subscribing in the mid-'90s. The arrival of the magazine has been a treat ever since. It must be one of the longest running hard copy fanzines. Hats off to you all.'
Chris Griffin

'For the last 35 years The FOX has always been a much anticipated read. It was a sad day when I heard of its closure.
Our amazing football club has had its ups and downs over that time, but thankfully it is in a much better place than when you started in 1987. You will always be a part of the club's history. You should be very proud. All the best in your future endeavours.'   **Philip York**

'Sorry to hear of the final curtain call of The FOX. It seems to have been part of the fabric of Leicester City supporters for ever. Especially those of a certain age.
All the best for the future.'
Barrie Underwood

'So sorry to hear of the demise of the fanzine. I was just getting set to name my 'Villain of the Season' as the prat who was responsible for set piece coaching. Along with Peter Taylor and, of course, VAR. Looking forward to The FOX Annual.'
Irving Roberts

'A huge thank you for The FOX over the past 35 years – a fantastic achievement. I was 17 when I first started buying it, and I've always enjoyed reading your Editorial, with excellent balanced judgement. I'm lucky enough to be a long-term season ticket holder, who goes to the match with my dad and son. My son Ben has already seen us win the League and enjoys going to away matches with his mates now he is 16. Best wishes for the FOX Annual and your future ventures.'   **John Hyman**

'Thanks for helping an old exile keep in touch with our wonderful club. My first match was Manchester City (h) in 1957. I was 10, we won 3-1 and I was hooked! I went to most games in the brilliant 62/63 season and one day I'll send you a few stories from then. Well done, and thanks again.'
John Campbell

'Thanks Gary for everything. I loved reading The FOX all these years, right from issue No 1. Looking forward to the Annual, all the best.'
Jeremy Cramp

'I just wanted to say 'thank you' for sending The FOX to me for so many years. I think I first subscribed when I was working out in Saudi Arabia in the late 1980s. We have certainly had a journey since! I'm pleased that you are continuing in an albeit less regular capacity and I look forward to The FOX Annual. Best wishes to you and your colleagues. Up the City!'
Andy Waterfield

'You lot are going to be GREATLY missed. Thanks for all the laughs over the years. Up the City!'
Garry McCreadie

'Very sorry and sad to hear that The FOX has come to an end, but fully understand the reasons. You and your close team of regular contributors and helpers have done a great job in keeping it going and it will always be the best Leicester City fanzine and probably one of the best (if there's a better one I haven't seen it) nationally. Best wishes.'
Andy B

'Very, very sorry to hear you are finishing but fully understand why. Thank you very much for all the great mags over the last 30-odd years. You've been a constant companion through all the dark Double Decker days of the late '80s, to the sunny glades of being top of the Premier League.

Really glad you've decided to keep going with the Annual, which I hope will be coming out for years to come. Respect for all the hard work.'
Jeff Smith

'Just wanted to say thanks a lot for going to the trouble of producing The FOX for so many years. The club has come a long way since the Bryan Hamilton/David Pleat days when you started. Glad you're doing the Annual - a great idea. UP THE CITY!'
Chris Hinsely

'Thanks for everything! Always particularly enjoyed the interviews and 40/50 Something which is an understated classic!'
Chris Hulbert

'Well, time to call it a day, what a journey it has been. Never in our wildest dreams would we have imagined we could win the Premier League, especially the season after The Great Escape. Thank you for the entertainment and honest opinions over the years. I fully support your decision to make closure at this time. It seems right. Looking forward to the Annual, yours in LCFC...'
John Cawley

'I want to thank you for the great deal of pleasure that you have given me over all my years of reading The FOX. The first one I bought was the David Pleat 'Calling International Rescue' cover - No 12. I have a complete set since then and they have never disappointed.'
Mick Hardy

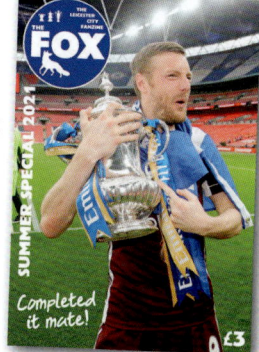

EDITOR

Today's mascot is Gary Silke who is ten years old and lives at 36 Main Street, Huncote. He attends Huncote Primary School. His hobbies are playing centre-half for Huncote Dynamos FC, judo because his mum makes him, basketball at Huncote Methodist Church, and collecting football stickers. His favourite players are Mark Wallington and Keith Weller. Good lad!
Other hobbies include producing The FOX fanzine for 35 years and writing a *Leicester Mercury* column until he got binned off during Covid.
New hobbies include Conker Editions Ltd who have produced 15 lovely books all about football that make great Christmas presents.

PICTURE CREDITS

Simon Kimber: front cover, 27, 30, 31, 52, 53, 59, 79 & 80. Plumb Images: 6, 7, & 52 (top left). Dave Morcom: 2, 21, 28, 31, 32, 33, 35, 37, 38, 40, 66, 69, 74, 87, 98 & back cover (Ian Ormondroyd). LCFC Archive/Bill & Avril Wood: 20, 60, 61, 62, 63, 64, 65, 82, 83 & 84. Neville Chadwick Photography: 39. Matt Appleby: 58. Russ Carvell: 86. Eddie Silke (me mam): 94.

ACKNOWLEDGEMENTS

Grateful thanks to everyone who has contributed to The FOX Annual No 1:
Simon Kimber for assistant editing, photography and setting up great interviews with ex-players; the talented Simon Smith, illustrator of FiftySomething (and the 28 year old Franz Carr strip!); Andy Wells for his piece on Admiral and his ammo box. Thanks also to Rob Coe, Chris Lymn, John Hutchinson, Derek Hammond, Ian Bason, and the Foxes Trust for their written contributions and to Clare Morris for hooking us up with any former-Fox who becomes a Ram, Matthew Mann for loaning us some of his LCFC memorabilia collection. And last, but definitely not least, everyone who entered the 1994 'Design a Kit' competition. In a way, you are all winners...

TEAMWORK

Grateful thanks to all our subscribers...

Neal Hurst | Richard Pole | Anthony Roe | Steve Anstee | Stewart Gee
Lance Tomlyn | Ross Tomlyn | Craig Tomlyn | Miroslaw Olszewski
Tina Wyngarde-Hopkins | Toby Coles | Charles Middleton
Stuart Teasdale | Laurence Goodchild | Tim Collison | Andy Collison
Ken Herts | David Evans | Jamie Snashall | Paul Jackson | Trevor Jolley
Nigel Wilby | Anthony Wilby | Richard Martin | K Langan
Marcus Muggleton | Steve Paine | Sören Filipsson | David Bevan
Andy May | David Squires | Stephen Pole | Wayne Barker | Mike Seal
Adam Behagg | Bill Shelton | Jon Follows | Ian King | Rob O'Donnell
Peter Johnson | Ian Mason | Jeremy Richards | Mollie Murrant
Lydia Murrant | Leo Murrant | Baily Murrant | George Goble
James Johnson | N Cruickshank | Chris Wellman | Duncan Bourne
David Layhe | Gavin Musson | Paul Kirk | Nick Fordyce | John May
Mr JA Johnson | Steve Haynes | Peter Smith | Helen Boyall
Nigel Wright | David Buckley | John Kasperek | Martyn Knott
Mick Envis | Alan C Mayes | Chris Courtney | Nicholas Beck
Andy Cassie | Robert Bracegirdle | Chris Upton | Malcolm Kisby
Edward Thomas | David Granger | Ian D Smith | Bryan Fisher
Peter Burrows | Philip York | Steve Hitchcox | David Wallwork
Nick Bonser | Adrian Hyde | John Bradshaw | James Martin
Richard Pyatt | Robert Danson | Neil Mason | Sophie Brookes
Chris Barkby | Ian Johnson | Keith Gutteridge | Michael Joseph
Michael O'Brien | Richard Stanley | Chris Holmes | Martin Clark
Angela Clarke | Tim Bowley | Chris Griffin | Jeff Richards | Filbo65
David Guest | Barrie Underwood | Irving Roberts | Ann Holyoak
Robert Pressler | Gavin Jacklin | Phillip Chick | Darren Hankey
Bill Brennan | Ian Middleton | Dave Johnson | Peter Read | Lee Fox
Brian Austick | Martyn Wilson | John Hyman | Keith Mason
Michelle Smith | Phil Sykes | David Henig | Marilyn Roberts
Chris Quinn | Paul Towers | Thomas Beavin | The Gavriel Family

Paul Russell | Peter Humphrey | RW Gascoigne | John Campbell
Jeremy Cramp | Rob Carroll | Mike & Julia Plant | Phil Hawtin
David Toone | Natalie Telfer | Nick Jelley | N C Goodfellow
Nigel Cook | John Pasiecznik | David Newman | A R Johnson
RE Johnson | Paul Marcus | Henry Ward | Michael Davies | Ian Croft
Dominic Lodge | Tony Duric | Andrew Waterfield | D McGrath
Brian Leitch | Daniel Payne | Richard Payne | Matthew Payne
Jay Barkus | Richard Cave | Andrew Moore | Henryk Cynkar
Mark Osborne | Mark Leonard | S Richardson | Richard J Sherriff
Sally Copeland | Paul Foulkes | Chris Lymn | Stuart Bushell
Dann Callis | Beau David Chesney | Jonathan Leigh | Rajendra Lal
Ian Wharton | Garry McCreadie | John Lunson | Bruce Anderson
Adrian Harris | Chris Walker | Simon Curley | Paul Jolley | Tim Edson
Rob Lagor | Steven Burgess | David Burgess | Karen Burgess | Tim Bird
Iain Smit | Janet Neale | Adrian Hill | Patrick Mannion | Ian Clements
Neil Aldred | Geoff Peters | Christopher Cooke | Alexander Ward
Andy Hulbert | Andy Buckingham | Nigel Horsley | Chris Ward
Jeff Smith | Michael Smith | Keith Laker | Steve Walton | Brian Lee
Caroline Neale | Richard Rumsey Adam Rumsey | R Neville | Phil Hall
Colin Lee | David C Parker | Tony McMahon | Andy Betts | R Hill
Eddie Criglington | Malc Clarke | Graham Tracey | Richard Rawlinson
Mark Peachey | Andrew Hodgkinson | Matt Maher | Jonny Carruthers
Chesfoxbooks | Derek Baker | Richard Fear | Richard West | Roy Jones
Colin Woodford | Paul Leeson | Hayley Gunn | Andy Wilkinson
Ian Lapworth | Dave Murray | Sharynn Mackay | Paul Martin
Peter Coles | Andrew Buckingham | Mark Buckingham | Daniel Pink
Graham Carruthers | Julie Bamford | David Allsopp | Andy Massey
David Parker | Will Parker | Billy Dunn | Daniel Hunt | Ian Cassie
Mark Buckingham | Andrew Winter | Gary Lovell | Ady Martin
Chris Hinsley | John Broughton | David Arch | Mike Tomlinson
David Smith | Andy Potter | David Joss Buckley | Michael J Smith
Nicholas Morritt | Mick Hardy | Tim Carvell | Wayne Gough

Chris Hulbert | John Cawley | Chris Swistak | Roman Rataj | Carl Klan
Martin Spencer | P Sharp | Thomas Hartwell | Glenn Brooks
Anatol Martschenko | Grainger Oliff | Tom Oliff | Gary Hurst
Nick Sharpe | Chris Kerslake | Ian Littlewood | David Lee Gilmore
Adrian Wilson | A D Buswell | Phillip Clark | Narinder Hayre
Malcolm Tedd | Michael Speight | Steven Postlethwaite | James Read
Nicholas Loney | Stuart Ettridge | Philip Passingham | Trevor Ringrose
Edward Holmes | Paul Evans | Michael Barker | Ian Cole | Andy Wells
Mark Crofts | Rob Waterton | Robert Coe | Rob Terpilowski
Stewart Henry | Max Henry | Noah Henry | Clive Billson | JM Corby
Philip Wright | Richard Merry | LW Newbold | Dean Redshaw
Simon Henig | Craig Moore | MJ Smith | Gareth Miller | Steve Scott
Gordon Quick | Ian Shaw | Reid Anderson | Brian Pick | David Riley
Kevin Hughes | Lewis Adam | Graeme Stevens | Robert McGregor
Mick Auton | Mick Butcher | Caroline Warrington | Andrew Morley
Rupert Whitlock | Adam Whitlock | Nigel Shier | Philip Bird
Martin Jarvis | Tom Scharenheuvel-Lewitt | Stephen Brown
Kate Langan - Foxes Pride Supporters | Elizabeth Biswas
Rob O'Donnell | Dylan Moverley | Gavin Musson | Ian Walton
Lloyd Glasgow | Paul Loftus | Anthony Sharman | Craig Booth
Dom Toth | Helen Boyall | Zoe Stevens | Aidan Gurr | Lee Lovett
Nicholas Hughes | Dave Parker | Will Parker | Ady Dayman
Wayne Pagett | Mick Andrews | Theresa Kendrick | Mike Wood